ACOUSTIC GUITARS
an illustrated history

ACOUSTIC GUITARS

an illustrated history

CHARTWELL
BOOKS, INC.

A QUANTUM BOOK

This edition published in 2010 by
CHARTWELL BOOKS, INC.
a division of BOOK SALES, INC.
276 Fifth Avenue Suite 206
New York, New York 10001
USA

Copyright © 2010
Quantum Publishing Ltd

All rights reserved.
This book is protected by copyright. No part of it may be reproduced, stored
in a retrieval system, or transmitted in any form or by any means, without the
prior permission in writing of the Publisher, nor be otherwise circulated in any
form of binding or cover other than that in which it is published and without
a similar condition including this condition being imposed on the subsequent
publisher.

QUMAGAI

ISBN-10: 0-7858-2596-7
ISBN-13: 978-0-7858-2596-8

This book is produced by
Quantum Publishing Ltd
6 Blundell Street
London N7 9BH

Publisher: Anastasia Cavouras
Project Editor: Valeria Kogan
Production: Rohana Yusof
Design: Loungefrog

Printed in Singapore
Printed and bound by: Toppan Leefung Printers Ltd

Content

Introduction

Yamaha Silent Series

The acoustic guitar as an instrument dates back over 4000 years, originating in what is now Europe and parts of Central Asia. First designs were constructed principally from animal sinew worked into string and stretched tightly over a wooden frame in order to enhance and project the created sounds. Evidence suggests that the guitar is older still, dating back as far as ancient Egypt and Babylon. The acoustic guitar has an enduring simplicity that belies the lifelong journey that is mastering its playing. There have been many to attempt the task of taming it, though very few have succeeded. Those who do succeed become music legends.

The guitar has traveled the world over, absorbing aspects of the characteristics of every culture and people it touches, gaining in craftsmanship and tone, and taking on new shapes as it does so. In our modern era of the 21st century, there has never been more diversity in the building, playing, and distribution of the acoustic guitar and it has truly taken on a world shape where it is recognized as a primary instrument in the genres of flamenco, rock & roll, and jazz amongst many others.

It has survived the advent of electronics, cheaper materials and result-oriented factories churning out sub-par instruments. How the acoustic guitar endures is a testament to the fine craftsmen and luthiers who have pushed the development of the instrument - from Japanese families dedicated to the building of musical instruments as a way of life, to the man in his California radio shop tinkering on his dream, to the seventeen year old fed up with the music industry - all have shaped the acoustic guitar in a very definite and tangible way. It is the seminal instrument of popular music leading into the modern era. Not one rock & roll song, not one popular arrangement of music is made without the acoustic guitar having laid the groundwork for it to happen years earlier.

The most exciting aspect of the instrument is where it is going, and how its past forms a foundation that every company and independent craftsman looks back upon and indeed depends on, in order to shape their future with the instrument. Throughout this work, we will examine many different acoustic guitars from a wide array of companies, showing just what each is doing to push the instrument forward, while still maintaining the true values of the acoustic guitar.

There are companies filled with traditionalists (those seeking to keep the guitar as it was created in the "Golden Era" of music), using time-honored materials and battle-tested working methods. Then we have those who continue to push the envelope, creating new woodworking procedures and experimenting with tonal woods that lie outside the norms of musical production. The resulting competition brings excitement for an instrument that has such a long and multicultural history and more importantly, shows that, even with the electric guitar having risen to prominence, the story of the acoustic guitar has much more still to be written.

MD95 Dreadnought with Spruce Top

The History of Alvarez

Alvarez has been building instruments, guitars in particular, since 1965. As evidenced by the sound and overall quality of their instruments, they are very passionate about their craft. The company continues the tradition of crafting guitars that have exceptional tone and durability by using an often abandoned approach in the face of a modern world. All instruments are designed by hand.

Now based in St. Louis, Missouri, The Alvarez guitar line (as it exists in its current form) began with a Japanese luthier named Kazuo Yairi who worked in partnership with an American company, St Louis Music (now LOUD Technologies Inc) to design their acoustic guitars. Yairi's family has a longstanding history of constructing the finest artisan instruments, and the company's current skilled luthiers continue this tradition.

Alvarez does not utilize more modern methods of guitar craftsmanship (such as computer technology and other high tech devices) to aid in the building process. They believe mass-produced guitars have a very uniform sound regardless of their original designer. With all Alvarez guitars being built by hand, each instrument is given its own spirit, unique tone and playability. The character of the instrument is able to shine.

The MD95 Masterwork

The MD95 Alvarez Masterwork features a breadth of tone and sweetness mixed with its rare value. Crafted using a traditional dovetail neck joint for greater resonance and stability, the MD95 features a modern thin neck profile to allow for greater access to the higher portions of the fretboard – this contrasts with its old-world construction to give the instrument its unique feel. The beautiful solid Indian rosewood back and sides on the MD95 bring subtle highlights out of the solid Engelmann spruce top. Indian rosewood is only available for purchase five times a year from its native country, further adding to the care and craftsmanship that is put into this acoustic guitar.

The breathtaking tree-of-life abalone inlay on the bound rosewood fingerboard complements the abalone rosette, maple body binding, bound headstock, gold die-cast tuners, and rosewood headstock veneer with abalone inlay.

The guitar is crafted in the dreadnought style, its larger body providing for greater resonance and serving to link its recognizable shape with many other acoustic guitar companies across the world. The MD95 was the flagship design of the Alvarez line for many years, and provides the basic framework from which all other masterwork dreadnoughts are constructed.

Famous Alvarez Players: Aaron Lewis (Staind), Ani DiFranco, Graham Nash, David Crosby, Pete Yorn, Seether, Duncan Sheik, Bob Weir.

Left: MD95 Dreadnought with spruce top Opposite Page: DYM95

DYM 85 Dreadnought with Satin Finish

Kazuo Yairi has dedicated his life to the crafting of the finest stringed instruments and every moment of that time, every glint of his expertise, is reflected in the Yairi Masterworks Series. The result is an instrument with a signature sound and distinctive look that harkens back to the birth of the acoustic guitar. What is most interesting about this particular design are the materials that go into its making, and how they pay homage to Yairi's homeland of Japan, where his factory is located.

The Materials of the Instrument

The DYM 85 Dreadnought features solid Kihada sides and back. Kihada is native to Japan, where it grows wild in the mountains. A deciduous tree growing up to fifteen meters (almost 50 feet) high, its outer bark is of a cork or buff color. In Japanese, 'ki' means 'yellow' and 'hada' means skin, which also serves to indicate one of the interesting features of the tree - once the buff or cork colored bark is peeled back, a bright yellow inner cortex is revealed. This inner cortex can be used for medicinal purposes, and the bark is also used as a type of dye for the treatment of important papers such as marriage, death and birth certificates (as the Kihada repels insects).

The selection of this wood in particular shows the depth with which Yairi considers the creation of his guitars. Materials make all the difference and ring the loudest when it comes to longevity of the instrument, vitality of its sound, and breadth of its appeal. When other guitar companies were expanding factory space and updating technologies in order to speed up building processes, Yairi was busy purchasing wood. His stores of North American spruce and cedar and, (increasingly rare) black ebony are to be envied.

A Note Regarding Tools

The tools that are used in crafting these guitars are important to note as well. According to Mark Meyers (a Yairi family historian), "The amazing techniques used by Japanese master luthiers in the manufacture of shamisens, (traditional Japanese stringed instruments), involved the use of cutting tools made from the same steel used to create samurai swords. These cutting tools were made from steel folded thousands of times in the founding process, and are considered legendary in themselves, simply because they are compared with the hardest steel ever produced."

The Instrument Itself

The 85 also sports a solid spruce top, a very commonly used wood for this particular portion of an acoustic guitar, as well as a very fine ebony fingerboard. The lack of electronics adds to the instrument's reputation as being "handcrafted". Its feel is understated, not intended for the flash of the stage or the pomp of fame, the DYM 85 has a true retro feel that almost seems to defy the term. Yairi has managed to craft an original instrument using materials from his home in Japan that show the global aspects of the acoustic guitar.

Yairi's brilliant design innovation has an extended neck tenon for a wider range of rod adjustment and does not include any neck/body irregularities. A unique coupled bridge design removes the forward pull from the bridge itself, allowing for greater stability and lighter bracing, leading to freer tone.

Above and opposite page: DYM 85 Dreadnought with Satin Finish

Blueridge

BR-160 Historic Series Dreadnought

The Founding Principles

Blueridge guitars are reminiscent (replicas) of the instruments built in the early 1900s. In the 1920s, The American fretted instrument industry was entering a Golden Era of craftsmanship and quality, producing many of the intricate instruments that would become some of the most sought after pieces for the modern guitar collector.

Unfortunately, factories were partially mechanized in their construction techniques, but every manufacturer still attempted to inject a portion of artistic handwork into the process. While it is a far stretch to the mass-produced acoustic guitars of today, it does serve to show the effects of the Industrial Revolution and mechanization on hand-crafted instruments, as well as the attempts by artisans (such as Yairi) to preserve their techniques by shunning technological advances.

The Construction Methods

Today, each Blueridge is still made with much the same methods as its classic counterpart in the 1920s. Artistic handiwork is evident in the well shaped, slim necks and the hand carved, parabolic "forward-X" bracing pattern that provides for greater expression in tone and volume. The similarity to earlier construction methods is most evident in Blueridge's pearl inlaid designs in the pegheads and fingerboards of each of their instruments. These original designs are made to look like they came from the 1920s, and are intended to capture the style and spirit of the Golden Era.

As with other acoustic guitars of the early 1900s, each Blueridge has the traditional dovetail neck/body joint and each model's neck features an adjustable truss rod. The truss rod was invented to allow a player to adjust both the tension of the fretboard and the distance of the strings from the sound port. This is used exclusively in steel stringed instruments to maintain the integrity of the wooden components and to prevent bowing. The Kluson style (a modern addition) enclosed tuning machines with "butterbean" buttons in either gold or nickel, which add a vintage feel. Blueridge guitars were created with the throwback model in mind, and the company prides itself on their careful attention to detail.

The Pre-War Look

The Blueridge BR-160 is a pre-war (1900-1920) inspired Herringbone dreadnought that is well constructed. The BR-160's classic design and ubiquitous sound are what has made it one of the more popular and affordable acoustic guitars currently in production. Readers of Guitar Player Magazine ranked the Blueridge BR-160 as #3 in a recent poll regarding acoustic guitars on the market today - a testament to this guitar's playability and endurance.

The BR-160 dreadnought features a select solid spruce top with hand-carved parabolic braces in the authentic pre war forward x pattern. The sound of the BR-160 is distinctly American, effectively recalling the Bluegrass period that its throwback feel is intended to evoke. Its construction illustrates the company's intentions to preserve the styles of a simpler time, when instruments were crafted to be more light and resonant.

Opposite page: Blueridge BR-160 Historic

Right: Blueridge BR-180 Historic

Blueridge

BR-143CE- Historic Series Dreadnought

The Blueridge BR-143 Historic Series 000 Acoustic Guitar illustrates the company's versatility in creating retro designs. Its smaller body size makes use of the instrument much simpler, in comparison to the larger dreadnought body styles of the early 1900s.

Crafting Methods

This guitar is crafted with a select solid spruce top, hand-carved X-bracing, choice solid mahogany back and sides, and a traditional dovetail neck joint. The intricate pearl and abalone inlay work on the headstock, fingerboard, and delicate marquetry center strip on the back are a signature representative of the original artist. Aged-tone finish completes the BR-143CE guitar's vintage look. The slim mahogany neck and comfortable 000-sized body work have the smaller player in mind, who would otherwise have difficulty handling the essentially lap-driven larger body styles. The cutaway of the body grants greater access to the fretboard, also making it ideal for the smaller player.

Blueridge Historic Series Guitars offer authentic vintage style with strict (sometimes predictable) adherence to the spirit of prewar instruments, from the materials used, to the ornate inlay work. While price is not a concern for many guitar players, Blueridge has been able to build instruments that feature the quality look of an earlier period without the price increase of a collector's item. Blueridge guitars are made with the same techniques as their antique counterparts, including many of the processes still being done by hand.

Important differences and Improvements

It is also important to note the hybrid aspects of these particular instruments. Like the majority of the guitars in Blueridge's acoustic line, while they are built to maintain the look of an earlier period, they do bear modern improvements. The 143CE is an acoustic/electric that has a pick-up installed which can be plugged into an amplification system. This, of course, was not available anywhere in the 1900s. A purist may consider these elements a cheat, but to any player wishing to take a performance to the stage, it's nearly mandatory.

Like other quality musical instruments, Blueridge guitars such as the BR-143CE acoustic-electric, are not built to over stimulate the viewer with aesthetic amenities. Meticulous attention to detail and quality craftsmanship is evident in the traditional, forward-position, hand-carved parabolic X-bracing which allows the solid spruce top to ring loud with great resonance. Blueridge guitars feature a traditional dovetail neck joint (all are similar to the BR-160), slim mahogany neck, adjustable truss rod, and butterbean-button, Kluson-style tuning machines, with an updated mechanism for modern precision and feel. As a company, Blueridge serves to maintain the traditional North American style of guitar. Their guitars often circulate among newer guitar players who wish to learn where they have come from, and what their origins may have sounded like.

Breedlove

Nylon Nouveau

A note about tone woods

"Why is it that different woods are used for acoustic guitars, and how do these woods affect the sound of the instrument? In the past, there was less opportunity for confusion on this issue, since most guitars were made of mahogany, rosewood, maple, ebony, and spruce. But with the dwindling availability of traditional tonewoods, particularly those cut from old-growth forests, major manufacturers and smaller luthiers have been compelled to consider the use of alternative species of tonewoods- some of them common and others decidedly uncommon." –Acoustic Guitar Magazine, March/April 1994.

It is this search for alternative tonewoods that birthed the Breedlove Guitar Company, an organization seeking to expand the traditional elements of acoustic guitar construction with new flare, and innovative design. Located in the lush countryside of Bend, Oregon, Breedlove has great access to different building materials.

"Top woods are usually softwoods coming from Gymnosperms, or conifers," writes the Breedlove Custom Shop, "Gymnosperms grow tall and straight, and have external seeds. The best top woods are very light, strong and stiff. Occasionally, a harder wood species (mahogany, koa, walnut) might be employed for a guitar top. Back and side woods generally come from Angiosperms - broad-leafed trees that bear seeds (fruits or legumes) in ovaries. These trees tend to be broad, with shorter trunks, yielding wood that is very strong and extremely heavy. Various hardwoods resonate at different frequencies. Some hardwoods vibrate and resonate for longer than others. Beauty, frequency range, and energy release characteristics make different back and side woods suitable for achieving a particular tonal goal."

Battling the U.S Economy

With only a few dealers per state, the biggest complaint from Breedlove customers is that they have trouble finding Breedlove guitars. Compounding this problem are economic factors making conservative retailers decrease their high quality musical instrument inventory in favor of faster selling, lower quality first guitars purchased by Guitar Hero fans and emerging school programs.

"We are reminding our retailers to sell (and consumers to invest in) quality that lasts a lifetime. Nothing feels better than finding the perfect instrument and knowing it will last. Also, online sales are growing but we believe that knowledgeable bricks & mortar dealers are still the foundation of the guitar culture" says President, Peter Newport.

Nylon Strings for the 21st Century

Designed to meet the needs of the modern player, all Breedlove Nylon String Guitars offer a heightened level of playability and flexibility. The Nylon Nouveau does so with a style that has come to be synonymous with the Breedlove name. Walnut binding serves as the border between the myrtlewood back and sides and the select Port Orford cedar top. Abalone Linear Fusion inlays guide the player's hand up and down the 14-fret Honduran mahogany neck.

The wood selection here is key as it displays the ideals of Breedlove - their ties with tradition and their break from the norms of guitar craftsmanship. In the face of dwindling supplies of wood, Breedlove has discovered a newer palette with which to push the creativity and innovation of the acoustic guitar.

Above: Jeff Tweedy of Wilco performs in support the bands' Wilco (The Album) release at the Greek Theater on June 27, 2009 in Berkeley, California

Acoustic Guitars: An Illustrated History   17

Breedlove

The Phoenix

The instrument

Building world class instruments with unique and exotic tonewoods is the strength of the Breedlove Guitar Company. Coupling a redwood top with ziricote (a South American dark wood) back and sides, the Phoenix produces a smoky, dusky tone that accentuates the ease of its playability. The Phoenix has an inlay of gold pearl, abalone and bloodwood, and the image of the mythical Greek firebird rises from the ebony fingerboard, which complements the bloodwood binding and herringbone top purfling.

Bloodwood is hard and tough, used mostly in areas such as cabinetmaking, rather than in the construction of musical instruments. Breedlove's innovations in their choice of materials builds on the experimentations that luthiers from around the world (mainly in areas outside the United States) have been already been conducting for more than fifty years - first working with what is readily available, then reaching out to more innovative materials and methods.

Ziricote Guitars

According to Allied Lutherie, Ltd, Ziricote is a wood that, "In appearance it's like some of the old Brazilian rosewood with spider webbing, 'volcanoes', and 'panoramas,' to use some of the descriptive terms used in reference to Brazilian rosewood. It is heavier than most of the rosewoods with a specific gravity of 0.95 and it tends to be a little brittle, and can split with a little provocation. It is a wood where the consistency of supply is tenuous." It is a reminder to all that resources in general, increase in scarcity with each instrument created.

But What Does It Sound Like?

"I think it was the '98 or '99 GAL [Guild of American Luthiers] convention that one of the amazing De Jonge family guitar builders, Joshia, had built a guitar of Ziricote that made other luthiers stand up and take notice," writes Allied Lutherie Ltd, "It was a quasi-blind listening test, that is, the builder of the guitar being played was not announced in advance. I've heard a few say that they were inspired to try Ziricote that day." As with all acoustic guitars, regardless of their construction, conventional or otherwise, traditionally constructed or mass-produced, tone is the greatest factor in determining the value and sustainability of the instrument.

Opposite page: Ryan Cabrera performs at the NBC Experience Store on July 1, 2009 in New York City with a Breedlove guitar
Above: a close of up Cabrera's guitar

España 55FCE

Nylon Strings 101

"Nylon strings" originated in ancient cultures and were used for the first stringed instruments. During those times, nylon string was built from animal gut and silk, though thankfully today we have less invasive methods of construction. Since 1935, synthetic polymer (first used in toothbrushes) has been used to create nylon strings for acoustic instruments, but that is where the current alternative to metal strings gets its name.

Acoustic Guitars that use nylon strings should never be strung with steel or nickel wound strings. Over time, the tension created by a steel string on an instrument designed to support only nylon will cause the guitar to warp, ultimately ruining it.

A Modern Take on a Classic

Cordoba Guitars was founded in 1997, and produces fine quality nylon string guitars. Though a relative newcomer to the industry, Cordoba houses some of the most accomplished luthiers in the world.

Since 1982, Edmund Blöchinger has handcrafted guitars from the finest quality woods, and has worked closely with the great guitarists of the Romero family (dubbed "The Royal Family of the Guitar"). Although he works alone and only produces ten handmade instruments per year, Blöchinger designs and oversees the building of all España, Artist, and Custom Artist level guitars made in Spain.

The Espana 55FCE is significant because of its electric crossover design, and was overseen throughout its production by Blöchinger. A spruce top is accentuated by flamed maple back & sides, sports a lacquered finish and European spruce for the soundboard. Its ebony fingerboard shows a commonality (or at least popularity) among the other stringed instruments being produced today.

Opposite page: a closer look at the Cordoba 55FCE
Right: the 55FCE headstock

The 55FCE flamenco guitar has a thin body with a cutaway and Fishman Prefix ProBlend electronics. With a quick, cutting sound and easy action, the Cordoba 55FCE is easily adapted for professional live performance. This is the benefit of electronics being added to the intimate ambience which may be created by using a nylon string acoustic guitar.

It is formally known as the "FCWE" and is a popular guitar that has been played for many years in Spain, where it was originally designed. Played by musicians like Donavon Frankenreiter and the Gipsy Kings, the 55FCE's thin body design, deep cutaway, and slightly narrower neck width give the guitar a comfortable feel at home, on stage, or in the studio. The Fishman Prefix ProBlend onboard electronics with 3-band EQ make the 55FCE the ideal guitar for improvisation with an amplified sound. The 55FCE and other similar hybrids are paving the way for innovation in such instruments, while still maintaining the core values of tone, quality construction, and artistry.

Cordoba players of note: Leonard Cohen, Bon Iver, Guster, Paolo Nutini, DeVotchka, One Republic.

14 Rose

What It Is To Be Truly Hybrid

The Cordoba Fusion Pro 14 "Rose" is a cutaway acoustic-electric guitar that features an all rosewood body (an increasingly rare material) with a natural finish, mother-of-pearl rosette and purling, and the B-Band A5T pickup system. This Cordoba guitar has been designed for optimization in both style and sound, hence the term "fusion." The Fusion 14 comes equipped with gold tuners with black buttons, Savarez 500CR Cristal Corum normal tension strings, and a Humicase classical size guitar case. The guitar was designed by Kenny Hill, an internationally recognized guitar maker, player, and teacher. Hill has been building guitars since 1973, and is currently the president of Hill Guitar Company, building nylon-string guitars for performers around the world. Hill is the chief designer and production manager of all Iberia and Fusion series guitars.

Cordoba Fusion models are nylon-string guitars for steel-string musicians. They are the first guitars to merge the acoustic bracing and tone of a traditional nylon with the thinner neck and fast action of a steel string. Radiused fretboards and 14-fret neck-to-body construction make these the most comfortable crossover guitars for steel string and electric players. The cutaway body style makes for easy access to the upper frets.

The B-Band A5T system features a slider 4-band EQ and volume control, notch filter and frequency rotary controls, phase button, low battery-LED, and full range chromatic tuner. The fully chromatic tuner has an LED strip that displays the note and individual LED's showing the half step, sharp, flat, and in-tune.

The Acoustic Guitar's Voice

Since the birth of the instrument centuries ago, lines have continued to become blurred. Here we are able to see the melding or hybridization of multiple cultures through the acoustic guitar from Japan, Spain, and North America - the sultry and seductive pluck of the nylon string acoustic guitar, merged with North American technology, in order to deliver it to a wider audience on a greater scale.

What remains the same is the sustained look and fascination with the guitar, its infusion into the global consciousness and its ability to show the sound of the culture that creates it. The similarities in construction, the use of ebony and Indian rosewood, nylon to steel strings, all continue to show the ubiquitous aspects of the instrument. The staying power of the acoustic guitar is evident in the way luthiers and craftsmen continue to make innovations, improve the technology and experiment with different tonal woods.

Three elements remain essential throughout history (modern technology notwithstanding) for the successful construction of a great acoustic guitar: wood, string, and people. The Trinity.

Adove: Cordoba Fusion 14
Rose detail
Opposite page: a closer look
at the Fusion 14 Rose

Butterfly Jumbo Acoustic

A newer marketing strategy

Daisy Rock Guitars was created in 2000 by designer Tish Ciravolo, with the intention of creating guitars specifically for girls. "As a longtime musician my experience has been that a guitar for girls is long overdue" writes the designer/ founder, "Standard guitars are often too big and bulky for the young female form. When I first started playing bass as a teenager, the instrument felt like a bat in my female-sized hands. At times, I wanted to quit because I felt like maybe the instrument just wasn't for me, or that I wasn't good enough to play it. I've encountered so many female musicians who have experienced the same set of feelings and I truly believe this is why we have a lack of female guitar-playing musicians in popular music."

Daisy Rock represents a departure from the more classic style dreadnought body that has come to be popular with male musicians. The company in particular is working through charitable organizations to swing the pendulum to a more artist-centric field and remove the masculine shadow over the craft of guitar making and marketing. Ciravolo has been aggressive in her strategy to get her company's message to the public and keep it in their consciousness. Daisy Rock as a company has had a presence at The Women's International Music Festival, sponsored the Bay Area Girls Rock Camp, The Southern Rock & Roll Girl's Camp, and the Girls Rock Vegas Day Camp, among many others.

The sound of the Jumbo Acoustic

The Daisy Rock Butterfly Jumbo acoustic-electric guitar features a bubinga, or a zebra wood body and a set mahogany neck. Bubinga is an African rosewood. Rosewoods are some of the most common tone woods used in the creation of modern acoustic guitars and serve to give the Butterfly its deep red color. The zebra wood model carries the lightness and deep dark lines of the wood's namesake.

The line boasts elegant butterfly inlays on the fretboard and headstock, white binding, and custom chrome tuners with the Daisy Rock logo. The guitar has a Fishman Piezo System for a competitive plugged-in tone. Nicole Solis writing for Acoustic Guitar Magazine said this in 2009 when reviewing the Butterfly Jumbo Acoustic, "…when I strummed more contemporary music, the Butterfly really shone. The rich, lasting sustain made open-string chord progressions absolutely swoon-worthy. As I went through the contemporary female singer-songwriter toolbox of muted bass notes, half-muted chords, and full-volume strums on songs by Terra Naomi, Aimee Mann, and, yes, Daisy Rock player Miley Cyrus, I found the Butterfly exceptionally responsive. I effortlessly brought the guitar from quiet, sensitive chording up to full-volume strums."

This shifting paradigm from male-centered instruments shows the guitar's continuing path as a sign of cultural shift. Just as it seems to take on the aspects of each nation or people that adopt it, the guitar is also adaptable to many cultural movements and works even here as a symbol for equality, something that retains its most basic elements (wood, string, people) while being able to also suit differing groups.

Opposite page: Butterfly Jumbo guitars from left to right: Bubinga Butterfly and Zebra Butterfly
Left: the headstock from the Butterfly Jumbo series

Daisy Rock Girl Guitars

Pixie Acoustic/ Electric

An anonymous letter to Daisy Rock Guitars

"I thought I was the only woman in the world with "music store anxiety syndrome" until I read Tish [Ciravolo's] story. At first I was happy to know I wasn't alone. Soon the relief gave way to pure anger and determination. How could I feel so intimidated patronizing a music store? How could a woman of any age NOT be intimidated? I love the guitar, but the guitar industry has never given women the slightest consideration. We struggle with instruments that dwarf us and weigh us down. We stretch our small fingers over necks designed for the large hands of men and we select instruments with color ranges that could only appeal to the masculine…This line has given me new inspiration for the instrument I love. I'm determined to promote this line and the dealer in my area that carries it. Thanks Daisy Rock for turning the tide and inspiring me to rock on!"

Opposite page: Pixie Acoustic Silver Sparkle and the Wildwood Acoustic Bleach Blonde
Right: Pixie Acoustic Powder Pink

Giving the Ladies What They Want

Continuing their aim to produce guitars that appeal directly to the female player, Daisy Rock breaks from the traditional "wood colored" instruments with the Pixie Acoustic/Electric series. It features Daisy Rock's trademark lightweight body and slimmer, easy-to-hold necks. The Pixie highlights innate femininity and an uncompromised pursuit of quality, while targeting the female guitar player and her specific needs and wants. High end features include a mahogany neck with rosewood fingerboard, pearloid Daisy inlays, and D'Addario strings. Other quality amenities include Grover tuners for rock solid tuning, a custom Piezo pickup system, and 2-band active EQ.

Daisy Rock is continuing their push to create quality instruments that can compete with more established guitar companies (Martin, Gibson, Fender, etc). It is evident in their use of more advanced hardware, better materials and electronics that they are truly working towards that goal. With superstars such as Miley Cyrus playing a Daisy Rock guitar all around the world for millions of young girls to see, it's clear that this company is generating the power to compete.

"As the mother of two girls, part of my motive for creating the Daisy Rock is selfish," writes Ciravolo in the company's mission statement, "I want to be able to provide them with opportunities that I didn't have. If they want to pursue music, I want them to feel comfortable and capable. The Daisy Rock is a line of high-quality instruments that are attractive and are a perfect fit for girls. My hope is that they will help give them an opportunity to build their self-assurance through music."

The widening of the playing field is essential in order to create a more diverse musical palate which is representative of the many varied tastes and perspectives that cause people (women and men) to pick up a guitar and decide to learn to play. Daisy Rock Guitars takes the tradition begun by luthiers (predominantly men) centuries earlier and tweaks it, asking the question that may be on every young girl's lips as she tries to approach the instrument, "Where is the guitar for me?" One needs to look no further than Daisy Rock.

Dean Guitars

V Acoustic

A Brief History of Dean Guitars

Dean Guitars was created in 1976 by a seventeen year old named Dean Zelinsky, a luthier with strong connections to the Rock & Roll community and a desire to change the landscape of guitar design. Originally based in Chicago, Illinois, Dean has made a name for itself producing electric guitars that have caught the interest of the heavy metal and rock communities. Dave Mustaine (Metallica, Megadeth) and perhaps more famously the late "Dimebag" Daryl Abbott have ridden Dean electric guitars to great success. Only a small portion of Dean's production runs have been allocated to the acoustic guitar, though it has been steadily growing due to the strong sales of their electric lines. Dean Guitars is currently owned by Armadillo Enterprises, which also owns Luna Guitars.

The Dean V Acoustic

The Dean V Acoustic Guitar is something of a 'cheater', in that has features that are more commonly associated with electric guitars: a thin body, unique shape (nearly identical to its electric counterpart) and a swift playing neck. Surprisingly, it is made with the same top quality tonewoods (spruce top, mahogany back and sides) found in traditional acoustic guitars. The Dean T-Wing Soundhole and rosette add to the visual appeal and the built-in Dean Buffer Preamp with 3-Band Equalizer gives the player the knobs, twist and turntables of an electric guitar with the feel and impressions of an acoustic guitar.

What is unclear is the sustainability of that resonance. Whereas more traditional designs, such as the dreadnought, jumbo, and the classic project their sound over great distances, the V Acoustic is exclusively designed for the stage and with amplification in mind. A modern convenience, but how many of the strengths of the instrument would this cause to be sacrificed? Is the appeal of the traditional aspects of the acoustic guitar simply a matter of preference, or do acoustics just function better?

The sound of the instrument

Purists (such as those in the camp of Blueridge guitars) will undoubtedly say that the traditional, "Golden Era" instruments hold the greatest tone and lasting appeal. They might say the electronic driven instrument is a 'crutch'; that the true strength of the instrument lies in the intimate tones created by handcrafted acoustic guitars, not factory produced instruments on a mass scale.

Still, necessity breeds invention and Dean Guitars clearly seem to be filling a niche in the market for acoustic guitar buyers. With the V Acoustic in particular, it appears to be primarily electric guitar players who drive sales, as they do not want to give up the sleek playability and signature shape.

Dean Guitars

The Performer Series

A return to the traditional with the Perfomer

The performer series of acoustic guitars shows Dean's ability to craft instruments in more of a traditional shape. Its feel is easily recognizable to the player who has a comfort level with jumbo and dreadnought body styles, but provides a bit of pomp and flare that is Dean's continuing drive to strike from the norm.

The Performer is a "mini-jumbo" built with a slight nod to the electric guitar, in contrast to the V Acoustic, which seems to be more of an outright copy. A Florentine cutaway allows for access to the higher portions of the fretboard and carries a Dean Preamp along with a chromatic tuner. Traditional woods have been used as well as a spruce top, and a mahogany body with abalone detailing. The Performer is also available in a variety of color patterns and specifications, making it one of the most versatile lines (in terms of appeal) in Dean Guitar's arsenal.

A note about pricing

It should be noted that while a handcrafted instrument delivers high quality craftsmanship, sound, and life, it does so at a high price. The majority of the instruments covered thus far have a significant price tag when compared with that of the Dean models, which have been produced using modern technologies in a larger factory setting. Whatever the model may sacrifice in quality, Dean manages to make up for in price, as their acoustic guitars are more affordable than the competition due to cheaper production methods.

In an emerging global economy what seems to take importance is the ability of the individual company to consistently put their guitars in the hands of the player and then keep them there. This creates lifelong ownership, as the player will come to appreciate the quality that the company (Dean, for example) produces, and then when finances are more readily available, the player can graduate to a more finely crafted instrument. The Performer in particular, is produced to be that introductory instrument that allows a player to have a guitar with the Dean label on stage, or in their home. We can see that Dean's strategy is slightly different from other guitar companies (with the exception of Daisy Rock) that seek the professional player, the purist, or traditionalist.

Dean Guitars is the perfect example of a guitar company using modern technology to decrease its sale price for the average guitar player, allowing more young people to purchase perhaps their first instrument and make that instrument a Dean. What began with a very young luthier nearly forty years ago has now come to the masses (for good or evil) by the forward march of technological advance.

Dean Guitars

Above: Phil Campbell performing on stage on his Dean Exotic from nature

Exotic from Nature

Economical versus Playable

The Dean Exotica line is an attempt to experiment with tonewoods in a way that is economical for the average guitar player. Like the Performer series, the Exotica features a wide array of guitar makes to choose from: there are nearly twenty acoustic guitars and counting in this series. From koa to walnut to zebrawood, the Exotica line attempts to bring the variety of tonewoods and their looks to the masses with varying degrees of success. Here the techniques used in managing these woods are a small hindrance.

Like most Dean guitars, the Exotica line is composed of acoustic/electric hybrids, meaning they have active pick-up systems installed in their woods. While some work towards simple amplification, Dean Guitars employ a proprietary system for their signature look and sound. The guitar relies on the tone controls of the Pre-amp to arrive at its sound, rather than allowing the wood to speak as the instrument. The tonewood in the Exotica series of guitars applies little to the actual tone, and more to the look of the acoustic guitar.

The differences in Tonewoods

Whereas a company like Breedlove Guitars are known for experimenting in tonewoods without active pick-up systems, Dean Guitars is best known for utilizing electronics to keep the size of the acoustic guitars smaller, more slender and easier to purchase and produce on a larger scale. Many would argue that this is in stark contrast to the ideology that birthed the company so many years ago when the company just consisted of a dissatisfied teen luthier seeking to change the way the guitar looked and sounded, at its helm.

The Exotic series is comprised mainly of rosewoods that have long been the staple for producing both acoustic and electric guitars. For the guitar player seeking an affordable instrument, Dean Guitars has shaped itself as a company providing an attractive alternative to guitar makers outside North America. What is unclear, as the history of the acoustic guitar lengthens, is whether the push of electronics into the instrument will truly prove to be a benefit, or become a necessary evil in the face of dwindling wood supplies and increasing production costs.

The Departure of Dean

In 1991, Dean Zelinsky sold his company to its present owner Armadillo Enterprises. In 2008 he removed himself altogether from the guitar company he created, saying, "I can no longer attach my name to the reputation, quality and direction of Dean Guitars or its current objectives…I wanted to get back to what put Dean on the map originally—building high-quality instruments that shape both the image and tone of guitar players, from the beginner to world-class professionals." Later that same year Zelinsky announced in partnership with Jeff Diamant (Diamond Amplification) and Terry Martin, the creation of DBZ Guitars LLC, a guitar line that would be overseen and controlled directly by the luthier.

Epiphone

AJ-100

How the Company Came to Be

Epiphone was once its own company, created by the son of a Greek timber merchant in the early 1900s, and produced mainly mandolins and banjos. The company enjoyed great early success through smart business practices and quality instruments, and competed outright with many larger guitar companies of the early '20s and '30s.

These days it serves as the "more affordable" arm of the guitar juggernaut, Gibson, which bought the company in 1957 for $20,000. It is somewhat ironic that the current owner of the company was once its greatest rival, as, in the 1930s, Gibson designed instruments for the sole purpose of competing with the rival Epiphone.

Since that time, and under the financial wing of Gibson, Epiphone has crafted a name for itself in the guitar making arena as a semi-detached entity from its parent company, producing reissues of existing Gibson models, as well as creating lines of their own.

Much of Epiphone's modern credibility came in the form of a visit from Rock & Roll royalty in the 1960s, when Paul McCartney, George Harrison, and John Lennon each purchased a Casino model double cutaway electric guitar. The Beatles rubber stamp served to boost the production value of Epiphone's electric guitar lines, which had floundered in the face of its already strong acoustic guitar sales.

Classic Designs without the Classic Pricing

The AJ-100 is the most classic (if also the most simplistic) example of that quality of craftsmanship. Built from mahogany and spruce with a rosewood fingerboard, the AJ-100 gives a balanced tone within its jumbo size, weighing in just shy of a dreadnought body style. The appeal of the instrument is shown in its ubiquitous construction, its use of time honored woods and materials that call to either the beginner or the pro seeking an instrument without all the bells and whistles of more contemporary models.

This acoustic guitar is also one of the most affordable on the market today and bares outstanding versatility in its design, available in either an electric/acoustic model or as a barebones, no frills acoustic. Epiphone has managed a better marriage of quality and pricing without sacrificing so much that they turn the model into something of a toy. The AJ-100 is the model by which many players first begin the task of toughening up fingers, learning chord progressions and changes, at the same time beginning to determine which features they most enjoy in an acoustic guitar - the sounds they prefer, and ultimately how to form one of their own.

Brand loyalty is very important for many guitar players, some never touching another maker's guitar apart from the one they first picked up when they were young.

Opposite page:
Main image: Epiphone AJ-100,
Smaller images: Epiphone
semi acoustic / electic guitars

Epiphone

The Hummingbird

The fine art of crafting the remake

The Hummingbird was first introduced in 1960 in its current dreadnought body style. It remains largely unchanged save for its production location, Korea. Epiphone's version (the one produced in Korea) is the more cost effective model of the Gibson made classic, and is a perfect example of how Epiphone was used by Gibson in order to place more of their guitars in the hands of younger generations.

The look of the Hummingbird is instantly recognizable. The rosewood fingerboard and spruce top have become staples of acoustic guitar production and continue to serve Epiphone in the consistent output of one of the more popular acoustic guitars in their line. The hardware is chrome, a less expensive alternative than the pricier and more conductive gold, which is more popular in the pricier models.

Left: Epiphone Hummingbird acoustic guitar

Off-site production hazards

With mass production comes a new set of difficulties for acoustic guitar makers, and Epiphone's version of the Hummingbird is no less immune to these problems. Lower paid factory workers do not possess the assembly skills or share the same passion for guitar making as the luthiers that originally designed and built the instruments in their smaller shops. While the instruments are certainly cheaper to make and therefore may be offered to the consumer at a lower cost, what is ultimately sacrificed is the quality of the individual acoustic guitar in the name of producing higher quantities.

One Epiphone player, who purchased a Korean made Epiphone Hummingbird, had his entire wooden bridge split in half while attempting to change strings. It was discovered that the factory had neglected to use wood glue in the proper places during construction. They had glued the bridge directly to the finish of the instrument, rather than to the wood of the body. The resulting bond wouldn't have held up in a light drizzle. An experienced luthier taking the time and care to craft his instruments properly would most likely have not made this mistake. Someone standing in a large factory where the current model being constructed is just one of thousands coming off the line that day may be no less careful, but likely more prone to mistakes due to the crush of volume.

That is not to say that all factory produced instruments are of sub-standard quality and design. Epiphone has made a name for itself in the modern era of guitar production by delivering a product to the consumer that is both cost effective and consistent enough to maintain a type of brand loyalty among guitar players. A musician's search for the perfect tone and the right feel for all circumstances can continue on a near constant basis. That Epiphone has been able to rise from humble beginnings as an independent company, survive The Great Depression and thrive amongst guitar companies that have come and gone is testament that the player knows best. Purist, young rocker, country, or blue-grass - if the player likes the instrument, that's what they will play, all other opinions be damned.

Above: Nick Colionne performing on stage with a semi acoustic/ electric Epiphone

Epiphone

The Dove

The Sister of the Hummingbird

This acoustic guitar is another Epiphone remake of an original Gibson model. The Dove was first produced in 1962 immediately after the Hummingbird model had its first production run. The Epiphone version, of course, lacks certain amenities that were featured on the Gibson model which had to be abandoned in order to allow for more affordability in the instrument.

The pickguard features the model's trademark Dove design and is available in several different finishes. Mother of Pearl is not used with this model (as it is with the Gibson) and the hardware is once again of a more affordable chrome.

The Advent of the "Big Box" Music Stores

The neighborhood guitar shop in North America has been under attack in recent years by larger corporate entities selling high volumes of instruments and wider arrays of products: the Wal-Mart of the musician's world, Epiphone, Gibson, and other companies have been able to take advantage of higher capacity factories in other countries in order to allow for cheaper production costs that, in turn, can be handed over to the consumer. The result (in theory) is a higher percentage of sales and profit because the instrument is more affordable, and therefore more appealing.

The internet is also the playground of the warehouse style music stores, such as Musiciansfriend.com, a website which will ship an inventory of literally thousands of guitars (acoustic and electric), basses, drums, even recording equipment anywhere in the world, usually at a discounted price and with free shipping. That can be hard to compete with, particularly for independent, sole traders who can not even buy the raw materials for the same price as they cannot purchase the same volume. Guitar companies now have many outlets to sell their instruments, and a manufacturer with low production costs (such as Epiphone) may use that affordability to ride out any economical storm.

The problem with many of these instruments that are purchased online (and a problem that differs from the handcrafted guitars of companies like Blueridge and Breedlove), is that many of them require a degree of fine tuning once they have been purchased and are delivered to a musician's doorstep. "If someone comes in with a guitar bought online from one of those websites, I won't work on it, "says one guitar technician at a local guitar shop in the central portions of Pennsylvania, "That's their fault." Air travel, in particular, can also alter the guitar's tuning.

Speaking of Guitar Center

The smaller, independent guitar shops may have the last laugh. As the United States economy continues to wither, larger chains that depend upon higher volumes in sales have been forced to scale back their ordering in accordance with what they're selling. The smaller shops require less income to pay the bills, service every piece of equipment that they sell, and establish more of a comfortable presence in their community.

Bain Capital (founded in 1984 by former U.S presidential candidate Mitt Romney and two others) purchased Guitar Center in 2007 for 2.1 billion dollars. Since that time, their associates have been instructed to honor the purchase price on a given instrument only, not to haggle or allow discounting (discounts are now run through store wide sales campaigns). While Guitar Center maintains a staff of experts and technicians at each location, it is unclear if commission-based sales have remained a part of their payment scale for items/ instruments sold.

Left: Epiphone Dove replica
of the Gibson Dove
Above: The Gibson Dove

Epiphone

DR-200 CE

This Epiphone model is an acoustic/electric that derives much of its sound from its Piezo/Shadow P4 Pickup and preamp system. Its construction is composed of industry standard rosewood for its fingerboard, mahogany for the body and spruce for the top. The most important thing about the advent of acoustic/electric guitars is the influence of its pickup system, which influences the guitar's sound much more than tonal woods where they are included.

A basic explanation of electronic amplification

The guitar pickup is a transducer that captures metallic vibrations, and converts them into an electrical signal that leads to the sound coming through the guitar's amplifier. Piezo electric systems (like the kind built into the DR-200CE) have a very high output resistance, which can hurt their ability to hold an electric charge. The buffer-amplifier is necessary in most acoustic guitars (including this one) in order to maintain a full frequency response. Pre-amps mounted in the acoustic guitar are used to prepare the signal for amplification, reducing distortion and producing a cleaner tone through the amplifier. The result is a sound which is much closer to the actual tonality of the string being plucked.

"The drawback to acoustic amplification is the limitation on how much amplification can be naturally produced," writes electric guitar enthusiast Tom Watson for StratCollector.com, "Although the amount of amplification can be affected by such factors as the size of the acoustics' hollow body and the force by which the strings are plucked, the instrument has a natural upper limit that creates a handicap for musicians in situations where greater volume is needed. This proved to be the dilemma of many guitarists in the big band era of the 40's and early 50's. Even the large acoustic jazz boxes were unable to produce sufficient amplification to let the guitar to be heard at the right volume when competing with rhythm and horn sections. Electronic amplification provided the solution."

The appeal of the acoustic guitar

Intimacy and precision both lend themselves to the enduring appeal of the acoustic guitar. After all, how many popular songs have a special acoustic version that fans cherish more than the original? Eric Clapton's acoustic version of "Layla," or the Dave Matthews Band's cover of "All Along the Watchtower" are examples of the acoustic guitar creating a mood by giving greater intimacy to a piece of music, which might otherwise be lost in the distortion created by its electric brethren.

An acoustic is often the first instrument a guitar player puts in their hands, where he or she learns to approach chords, strings, the chops. What has not changed over time with the acoustic instrument is its ability to establish mood, show a player's ability, and be the instrument that players seeking to improve their craft will always return to. The acoustic guitar is an instrument whose sound comes down to more than the turn of wire on a coil, and can be dictated by the luthier's hand, and the choices of wood that go into its construction.

Opposite Page:
Main image: DR-200CE
Smaller images: DR-21S (left),
DR-200S (right)

Epiphone

Paul McCartney 1964 Texan

The Beatles strike again for Epiphone. Well, just one Beatle, really. The Texan is an Epiphone remake of the iconic guitar made by Gibson, and the one that McCartney used to record the Beatles' hit "Yesterday." This guitar is an example of the artist being involved in the guitar making process, as McCartney worked with Epiphone to ensure that the intricacies of the original instrument remained intact. Artist involvement is a significant help to guitar companies who have been encouraging "signature models" of their instruments (guitars popularized through their use by a given player). For Paul McCartney, the Texan is almost as identifiable with his image as his Hofner Bass.

The guitar retains its lacquered finish, Kluson machine heads, and (at the artist's insistence) was hand built by Gibson at their acoustic workshop in Montana. The 1964 Texan represents the first acoustic guitars constructed for Epiphone in the United States in nearly forty years. It is interesting that, while a company may have taken advantage of factory style production lines, when it comes to more artistic projects (such as restoring a vintage instrument), hand built is the way to go. Of course, this means the runs of instruments created are often limited, though this is also a choice made by design. Limited supply leads to increased demand. Even guitar players cannot fight Adam Smith.

The Limited Edition and Custom Guitar

The 'limited edition' is a concept guitar makers have been using for some time. In the beginning, it was more out of necessity than the desire to drive sales. A luthier only had so much time to construct a given amount of instruments, so scarcity was a natural consequence. With the advent of replaceable parts and conveyer belts, the "limited" (or custom) guitar as a concept had to be reintroduced. These editions are often based upon existing models that famous musicians use. McCartney has the 1964 Texan, just as Eric Clapton has a signature Fender Stratocaster, and so on. It gives the guitar player looking to sound like their idol the ability to do so, while being reasonably assured that they are getting a quality instrument in the process. Most artists take great care when attaching their name to a product so connected to what they do for a living.

The modern goal for guitar making may be summed up within two opposing ideologies. The side that is simply seeking to put a guitar in the hands of everyone that wants one, and the side desiring to produce a quality instrument using time honored practices, though this may often sacrifice affordability and the availability of the product. As we have said before, companies that produce more expensive, handmade instruments like Cordoba or Breedlove have expressed a sense of frustration at not being able to grab a wider audience for their products. The good rides shotgun with the bad in such cases.

If a child wants to learn to play, there is nothing wrong with a "starter" instrument to help them master the basics and develop a love for music. Epiphone produces a quality array of affordable instruments, which means that this desire can easily be fulfilled. When they become rock stars, they can afford to graduate to something a bit pricier.

Left: a closer look at the case and Paul McCartney signature Epiphone Texan acoustic guitar
Opposite page: Paul McCartney with his signature 1964 Texan guitar

Fender

Tim Armstrong Hellcat Acoustic

How Fender Started Out...

California is the birthplace of Fender Guitars, and also the home of its namesake, Leo Fender, who began making custom guitars in his own radio shop (then called Fender's Radio Service) in the 1940s. He sought to improve on the modified hollow body (acoustic) guitars that jazz musicians were using to raise their sound over the timbre of trumpets and saxophones. Early electrified hollow-body guitars gave off a great deal of feedback when played at high volume, and Leo thought he could improve on this.

In 1951, Fender introduced the Broadcaster, more of a prototype solid body electric that would eventually lead to the design of the Telecaster, an electric guitar that has become synonymous with the Fender name. The Fender Stratocaster would follow the Telecaster in 1951, and cement Fender as one of the most popular guitar makers of the modern era. Leo Fender did more than improve upon the electric guitar - he practically put it on the map. The company has had its ups and downs, from a sale to CBS, sinking into artistic limbo, and eventually managing to creatively right the ship. Fender has weathered enough storms to show it's made of the right wood.

An Acoustic Guitar for Punk Rock

Fender, as a company, has been producing acoustic guitars since the 1960s, and though the brand has garnered more fame for its electric instruments, their acoustics have benefited in that Fender is able to offer them at a more consumer friendly price. Not to mention the company's ability to attract a rock star or two to help them sell a guitar every now and again.

Tim Armstrong is the frontman for the iconic punk band Rancid, and his Fender model is the recreation of a 60's era acoustic guitar that Armstrong wrote the majority of his band's songs on. Just as Epiphone did with the Texan and Paul McCartney, Fender is using the marketability of Armstrong to provide an instrument to the public, created to his specifications. It gives the guitar instant street credibility with fans of the band.

The Hellcat features pearl acrylic "Hellcat" logos on the 3rd, 5th and 7th frets, chrome hardware, and twin skulls for the guitar's twelfth threat. Fender has also installed its signature FTE3-TN pre-amp (with built-in tuner) along with vintage style tuning pegs, into this very economical vision of Armstrong's original.

Mass appeal is something that punk rock has tended to resist since its unearthing from the undergrounds of Britain and the United States in the late '70s. An acoustic guitar would seem like a similar pariah, though one that seems to be so straight laced that it is revolutionary, and therefore punk rock. Good music trumps aesthetics, and it has often been said that the true test of any good song is whether or not it can be played on an acoustic guitar. The acoustic guitar has grown, even in areas of music which would seem to shun it - a rubber stamp for quality song craft.

Left: Tim Armstrong Hellcat guitar
Opposite page. detail

Fender

J5

The Artist and the Influence

Not the Jurassic Five, The J5 (John 5) is the acoustic guitar for the inner shredder in every musician – he is in there, just plotting. The J5's design was overseen by the artist who also has several other signature instruments available with Fender. The result is an acoustic guitar, which possesses well-developed tone, light-speed playability and terrific stage appearance.

John 5, born John William Lowery, has played with Marilyn Manson, Loser, Two, David Lee Roth, and most recently with Rob Zombie and Meatloaf. Manson gave him his stage name, as John was the fifth replacement guitarist for the shock rocker's band. He has also released several solo instrumental works. Fender has also produced a J5 Telecaster which bares a similar look to the J5 acoustic.

Features include a gloss black body with chrome pickguard, solid spruce top, mahogany neck, back and sides, chrome die-cast tuners, a Florentine (sharp) cutaway, John 5 Telecaster headstock and Fishman Classic IV T electronics with built-in tuner. This modern take on the traditional jumbo body style shows the benefits of the latest technology regarding preamps and tuners, but lacks the deep, velvet low tones of a handcrafted dreadnought or jumbo. It is clearly an acoustic guitar designed for the musical demands of the Rock & Roll guitar player.

Transition from Country to Blues to Rock & Roll

The rise of Rock & Roll as the dominant art form in music began as early as the early 1940s, and blues artists like Robert Johnson produced the architecture for what would become the basis of modern Rock & Roll. With the transition from a Country (bluegrass, folk) aesthetic to more of a blues-based Rock, came the need for a different instrument. For some it was the electric guitar (the route Bob Dylan famously took), and for others, it was to look at the acoustic guitar as an instrument that would be able to reinvent itself, adjust to the newer needs of a rock song structure emphasizing higher end notes, chunkier strumming techniques and tone over individual note clarity.

The J5 is an example of that adaptability in the same manner as the Hellcat Acoustic - whereas the Hellcat was built for a punk musician and, as such, emphasized the affordability and look of that acoustic guitar, the J5 sports higher end technology, increasing its sale value. However, the wood construction of the J5 is of a similar ilk (spruce, mahogany) as that of the Hellcat, and that is something that will never really change for the acoustic guitar industry, with the exception of those experimenting with rarer materials and more native tonal woods.

Opposite page: a closer look at the Fender J5 acoustic guitar

California Kingman 10

The sounds of the Left Coast

The Kingman is part of Fender's California series of acoustic/electric guitars. More electric than acoustic, the Kingman has Fender's signature Stratocaster headstock, thin neck style, and also sports a scalloped "X bracing," gold hardware, and Fishman Aero pickup system. The California Kingman is constructed in Fender's "tight" dreadnought body style with a slight cutaway in order to provide some increased access to the upper frets. In contrast to the staples of mahogany and spruce, this acoustic/electric is built with solid cedar for the top and rosewood (usually isolated to fingerboards due to its scarcity) for the back and sides, which gives the guitar a weathered, almost wind beaten look to it.

Opposite Page: Fender Acoustic Kingman and Fender Acoustic Kingman 10

This model is very new, introduced in 2009 and is intended to be a nod to the California series of Stratocasters that Fender produced from 1997 to 1998. This acoustic is part of the continuing trend by guitar companies to create vintage style (or 'vintage looking') instruments that contain modern electronics and materials. In a world where the old are quickly forgotten in the relentless march of what is sleeker and more optimal, the guitar (similar to instruments in general) is a symbol of the past still building and informing the present. As a foundation instrument for many guitar players, it does not get much more rock solid than the acoustic guitar, and Fender seems to be in tune with that sentiment.

The History of the X Bracing

First invented by the C.F Martin Guitar Company in the 1840s, X bracing is a system of construction in which two braces are set on the inside of the acoustic guitar in a literal X pattern. This allows for greater stability in the instrument and for more resonance or volume. Before this invention, acoustic guitars had been predominantly Spanish styled (classic) or nylon stringed and fan or parallel braced. These styles did not give enough support for the pressure demands of newer instruments. The X brace provided the necessary skeleton for an acoustic guitar to support steel or nickel wound strings without simply rattling apart.

The scalloped style X bracing that is featured on Fender's Kingman 10 is built to allow more vibration, bass resonance, and overall volume throughout the instrument. The scalloped bracing system is actually the older of two designs (scalloped, un-scalloped) and has been more popular with bluegrass musicians since its inception.

Fender is using this particular method of construction for tone, in order to give the Kingman that "California" sound - the relaxed tones of the coast, of open space and creative bustle, and also to compensate for the thinner body that is often the province of acoustic/electric guitars. A palm tree and setting (or rising) sun has been designed into the neck (Fender has dubbed it the "Polynesian Surf Glyph Rosette") of the guitar to give the player the impression of being close to the water and warmth.

CD 100

Speaking of classics, Fender has produced an acoustic guitar in a continuing vintage vein but in a classic style. The CD 100 has been built in a traditional dreadnought pattern, though Fender's CE 100 has the "slender dreadnought" body style that Fender has pioneered. The guitar is also available in either a right-handed or left-handed model.

The goal of the CD 100 is to put a Fender guitar in the hands of anyone that wants one, meaning that it is extremely affordable. The ability to create guitars that are both affordable and sturdy enough to justify the purchase has become the hallmark of larger companies (like Fender) who have the benefit of off-site factory production.

Honorable Mention Goes to the Amplifiers

The star of the show has always been the guitar, followed (if at all) up by the guitar's amplifier (to say nothing of the artist actually playing the instrument). Leo Fender, along with business partner Clayton "Doc" Kaufman, began building homemade PAs out of their repair shop in the late 1930s. Kaufman would eventually pull out of the partnership, leaving Leo Fender to produce and distribute his quickly growing homespun guitar and amplifier business.

It was touch and go at first for Leo, who still worked long hours at his repair shop, but by the late 1940s, his guitars had begun to acquire some credibility with performers and musicians across the country, thanks in part to a distribution deal he struck with the Radio and Television Equipment Co. Fender's initial amplifier was a chrome-laden piece of hardware that garnered a reputation as being something of a road warrior. It was heavy, solid, and held up well, bouncing around the country in the backs of vans and band buses. It was also the most powerful amplifier on the market at the time.

A newer model wasn't produced until Fender created the famous P-bass in the early 1950s, which required the invention of an amp that could handle the output of an electric bass guitar. The Bassman was created, and would actually go on to become one of the most often used amps by guitar players as opposed to bass players. Acoustic guitar players have used them to handle the deep bass and velvet tones created by dreadnought and jumbo body styles.

The reason for the Bassman's popularity was its incorporation of the tube amplification system - which has attracted many a guitar player since its creation. The circuitry has been changed by Fender many times over the life of the company, and the reasons for its technical appeal are complex. The appeal of the tube amplifiers comes from the fact that they are said to "sound better" the longer they're turned on (this allows the liquid or gas contained in the tubes to "warm up" and deepen the sound produced). Tube amplifiers are also capable of the highest electronic output available on the market. If there is a guitar amp out there with a knob that goes to eleven, it would have to utilize a tube amplifier.

Fender

GA-43 SCE Grand Acoustic

The GA-43SCE Grand Auditorium features a comfortable, resonant cutaway body with a Spruce top; rosewood back, sides and fingerboard and Fishman electronics. Accents include: Abalone dot inlays, Abalone rosette, bound fingerboard, rosewood headstock overlay, and tortoise shell binding. Chrome die-cast machine heads keep the price of the instrument low.

The Fender/Fishman Classic 4 ACLR pickup system features volume, bass, mid, treble, body (mid-sweep), and low battery indicator light. This gives the guitar player optimal control over the tone of the instrument once plugged in. As we have said before, electronics overpower a hybrid guitar over other choices in building materials such as wood. The latest models are also being sold with a hard shell case included.

How Fender is Moving Forward

Leo Fender, in poor health, sold the company to CBS, in 1965 for $13 million. There the company remained until 1985, when a small investment group lead by then Fender president William Shultz, bought Fender from the divesting media giant. At that time, all that Shultz and his associates had owned was the Fender name, patents for their instruments and whatever remained in stock - no warehouses, no factories.

At first, they attempted to use foreign guitar makers who possessed a reputation for generating quality product (guitars etc) at a high volume. After a short time, frustrations over off-shore construction quality of instruments lead Fender to establish a home base in their factory situated in Corona, California. The location remains Fender's center of American made guitars to this day. They have also built factories in Ensenada and Baja, Mexico, where more budget conscious lines are produced for Fender.

Business Savvy Strategies

Two years later Fender acquired Sunn, a legendary line of amplifiers used by such artists as Jimi Hendrix, Pete Townshend, and The Rolling Stones. The acquisition provided Fender the impetus it needed to jump back into an arena that had traditionally been one of its strengths; amplifiers. Shultz and his team simply slapped the Fender logo on Sunn's already established product line and gained the ground the wounded company so desperately needed.

Another area that kicked off in earnest around this period was the artist driven signature models. Fender recognized the consumer desire to own the instruments that had been constructed for their idols, and used this as part of their strategy to put things back together and stride confidently into a new era. Today's artist driven models such as those featured here, The Hellcat Acoustic, and the J5, are possible because of Fender's open door policy towards musicians. Fender has worked to create custom instruments and amplifiers for many professional musicians, including Eric Clapton, Elvis Costello, and Victor Bailey among many others.

The growth for Fender has been dramatic, if not flawless. Fender has come from not even having the facilities to produce its once proud roster of guitars, to manufacturing guitar accessories, a widening line of basses, electrics, and acoustic, amplifiers, and recording equipment. The Fender Musical Instruments Corporation is still helmed by the man that wrestled the company from CBS over twenty years ago, William Shultz.

Opposite page: Fender Acoustic GA-43 SCE Grand Acoustic

Overleaf: Dave Davies & Ray Davies backstage in dressing room at 'A Whole Scene Going' TV show, holding Fender Malibu acoustic guitar

Fender

F48 Steel Resonator

The sound of a steel guitar is unmistakable. Its unique twang and metallic slide notes are the mark of an earlier time, when bluesmen roamed the Deep South of America. A resonator is actually still an acoustic guitar, but one whose body is made from one or more metal cones, instead of wood boards that are found with a traditional acoustic instrument. The resonator was the initial answer from luthiers for guitar players who were having trouble being heard over big band instruments like trumpets and trombones. When the amplifier rose to prominence the resonator was mostly abandoned, though it still found a home with niche musicians in bluegrass and the blues players of the Mississippi delta.

Resonators were produced in two styles: a square-necked style designed to be played like a traditional guitar and, a round-necked style which could either be played as a classical instrument or a lap-steel guitar. One of three main resonator designs are usually built into steel resonator guitars: a single inverted-cone resonator used by the Dobro (made from metal and wooden parts) acoustic, a "biscuit" style cone utilized by National Resonators, and a tri-cone resonator style which was used for the first National Guitars.

The Inventor

John Dopyera was the first to design the steel resonator guitar in the early portion of the 1900s. He did so at the request of musician George Beauchamp, whose complaint was similar to other musicians of that time period: big bands were drowning his sound out. Beauchamp would go into business with Dopyera to manufacture and distribute the luthier's instruments under the National String Instrument Corporation. Dopyera would end up leaving the company less than a year after it had formed to start the Dobro Manufacturing Company, whose name became the gold standard for steel resonator guitars.

Fender's Take on the Resonator

The F48 is built from chrome steel, rosewood (fingerboard) with custom "F" (for Fender) sound holes. The guitar is built with the average guitar player in mind who might be seeking to add a resonator style acoustic to their arsenal, and, as such it does not carry all the bells and whistles of a higher end (wood bodied) resonator.

Weight is the first identifiable feature in a resonator, and is no less the case with Fender's model shown here. It also lacks electronics of any kind, which is more a safety requirement than a result of purist tendencies; an all-metal guitar is not an ideal candidate for an electric current. Fender does feature wooden style resonator guitars with a pickup system, but one is not available on the F48. The guitar also sports a smaller number of available frets than a traditional acoustic guitar. The F48 Resonator has nineteen available frets whereas the majority of dreadnoughts and jumbo acoustics built today have twenty to twenty-two. All this adds up to a diminished higher register of notes for the steel resonator - though this instrument was hardly designed for screaming solos.

Left: Fender F48 Steel Resonator

JG12CE-12 (12-string)

How the instrument works

The strings are placed in rows of two strings each that are usually played together. The two strings in each bass or lower portion are normally tuned an octave apart, while each pair of strings in the treble courses are tuned in within the same octave. The tuning of the second string in the third course (G) varies: some players use a unison string, while others prefer the distinctive high-pitched, tolling quality that an octave string makes in this position. The resulting sound is a shimmering quality, deeply textured and layered with lilting high notes.

Some players, either in search of distinctive tone or ease of playing, will remove some of the doubled strings. For example, removing the higher octave from the three bass courses simplifies playing running bass lines, but keeps the extra treble strings for the full strums. The versatility of the twelve string acoustic guitar is readily apparent.

Left: Fender JG12CE-12 acoustic guitar.

The tension placed on the instrument by the strings is significant, and because of this, twelve string guitars have a reputation for warping after only a few years of use. Advances in truss rod construction have worked to correct this problem, and some twelve string guitars are being built with non-traditional structural supports to prevent or postpone such a fate. This is done at the expense of appearance and tone. Until recently, twelve string guitars were nearly universally tuned lower than the traditional EADGBE, to reduce the strain on the instrument. Melissa Ethridge, a famous user of the twelve string acoustic, has often been said to tune her guitar a half step down to E flat.

Fender's Design for the Grand Concert

The JG12CE-12 is a twelve string mini-jumbo acoustic-electric guitar that creates a sound not unlike an orchestra. It is a point in favor of Fender's design team that the guitar still plays comfortably. The task is made easier, thanks to its elegant Venetian (soft) cutaway which allows the arm to slide around the guitar more easily, as well as granting greater access to the fingerboard. Features include a spruce top, mahogany back and sides, nato neck, rosewood fingerboard, chrome die-cast tuners and Fishman Classic IV electronics.

The twelve string is the acoustic guitar of the one-man show, the performer that needs to sound like a choir and often has the vocal prowess to back it up. The Jimi Hendrix Experience used a twelve string acoustic to back up a soaring Stratocaster on the band's cover of "All Along the Watch Tower", Jimmy Page famously wrote "Stairway to Heaven" on a twelve strong acoustic to compliment the wailing vocals of Robert Plant, and Tom Morello of Rage Against the Machine has often employed the instrument during live performances, just to name a few. Since its resurrection from obscurity with the progressive rock of the late 1970s, this guitar model has shown staying power, if only for its dramatic visual appearance and theatricality it usually garners when brought on stage.

While it does carry the hazards of its tuning routinely breaking down, or strings snapping at the lightest increase in tension, clearly the twelve string acoustic guitar has a place of great appeal for the modern rock songwriter and performer.

Above: Jimmy Page of Led Zeppelin performing live onstage, playing acoustic guitar

Gibson

J-45 Standard

Standard is a word that has several meanings when applied to Gibson's J-45 acoustic guitar. It is of simple construction, very much a "standard" slope-shouldered acoustic dreadnought, first produced by Gibson in 1942. The J-45 has been nicknamed "the workhorse" - for its durability and for being Gibson's best selling, most popular acoustic guitar since its creation. Originally built to compete with C.F Martin & Company's "D" line of guitars, its simple elegance and playability is the industry standard for quality and sight recognition.

Premium Sitka Spruce makes up the top as well as the hidden top and back braces. Honduras Mahogany is used to construct the sides and back of the body and neck. High quality Indian rosewood is used to create the bridge and fret board. In accordance with its simple motif, mother-of-pearl dots flow down the fret board and a plain, teardrop shaped pick guard protects the top. Nickel Grover's original Rotomatic tuners are an engineering marvel, with abundant style and performance, exactly suited for the J-45. With a gear ratio of 14:1, the Rotomatics deliver precision tuning in a durable housing that provides maximum protection for the gear and string post. All moving parts are cut for exact meshing, eliminating the possibility of slippage. A countersunk tension screw allows the musician to regulate the tuning tension to any degree. A special lubricant inside the gearbox provides smooth and accurate tuning stability.

Continued Use of the X Brace

Every acoustic guitar made by Gibson features hand-scalloped, radiused top bracing inside the body, a feature normally found only in limited run, hand-made guitars. By scalloping each brace by hand, the natural sound of the acoustic is focused more toward the center of the body, enhancing the instrument's sound projection. The Gibson J-45 Standard guitar features a variation of Gibson's "X" bracing pattern situated behind the soundhole (as we can see every guitar company claims to have invented the X brace), with a set of tall and thin braces for the back, and scalloped tall and thin braces for the top. This ubiquitous bracing design (seen earlier with Blueridge Guitars and Fender models) delivers a balanced expression, with punchy, deep lows, warm mids, and clear, crisp highs. When pushed for more volume, the Gibson J-45 projects a natural compression, which helps it blend well with any accompaniment.

The Artist's Perception of Quality

While outwardly simplistic, the reason for the J-45's popularity rests with the materials used in its creation and this is reflected in the instrument's pricing, which may be viewed as considerable for the guitarist first picking up the groundbreaking acoustic. It is the unfortunate cost for quality in a global economy where large factories are able to out produce smaller ones, thereby increasing visibility in retail markets. Fortunately, guitar players are not easily fooled and have a keen eye for detail and a winning tradition. The J-45 is the 'little black dress' of the guitar world: constructed with the best materials, simple in style, and compliments nearly everyone that puts it on. This acoustic guitar will never go out of style.

Opposite page: a closer look at the Gibson J-45 Standard acoustic guitar.

Gibson

J-45 Legend

The Gibson J-45 is one of the most played and cherished acoustic guitars in history. It is also the guitar that First Lady Michelle Obama presented to Carla Bruni-Sarkozy (the wife of the French President) during the Obama's first 2009 European trip. This Gibson Legends version of the J-45 guitar handles music from the blues to bluegrass, to folk, to pop, and has the work history to back up its lofty claims. Hand crafted by Gibson luthiers using techniques from the J-45 guitar's initial creation in the early 1900s, the Legend J-45 boasts an Adirondack spruce top and solid mahogany back and sides to produce unmatched mellow, full-bodied tone.

The Challenge of Reproducing the Original

The J-45 Legend is the result of Gibson luthiers (located in Bozeman, Montana) searching for and then discovering a vintage 1942 J-45. The guitar was owned by acoustic guitar expert and author Eldon Whitford, who was gracious enough to allow the luthiers at Gibson to examine the instrument. The guitar went through both X-Ray and CAT scans in order to accurately determine the bracing patterns and wood thickness. The glue and finish were chemically analyzed. To make a long story short, Gibson learned everything he possibly could about that guitar, and the result is the J-45 Legend, which attempted to recreate the way the original luthiers first crafted the inaugural J-45.

The body of the guitar is constructed of solid, premium grade Honduran mahogany, and the top is solid Adirondack spruce. Both the top and back are gently radiused to provide tension to the wood. This makes the wood vibrate (similar to a tuned drumhead), and as a result, projection and definition are greatly enhanced. Hot hide glue is used in the construction, not synthetic glue, which is used in many of today's factory produced guitars. Hide glue is organic, and thinner - it makes for a better wood-to-wood construction, without a thick layer of adhesive to impede the guitar's vibration. The lighter the adhesive materials a luthier can use, the better.

The top bracing is exactly like that of the original, all carved and shaped by hand, with even the tooling marks still present, just as they were in 1942. The lightweight, wide "X" bracing ensures a guitar top that vibrates easily and produces a sound that is well sustained. The reissue J-45 guitar's fingerboard is (increasingly) rare Madagascar rosewood, graced with vintage style frets, .082" wide by .093" high. The fingerboard also has mother-of-pearl dot inlays, just like the original, and the bridge is Madagascar rosewood as well. Both the nut and saddle are bone in order to maximize string vibration transfer.

Handcrafted construction seems to be disappearing from the guitar world. Wood is disappearing at an alarming rate, and synthetic materials are becoming more of a necessary evil than a means to increase profit margin. Indeed, the J-45 Legend's price tag is nearly triple that of the J-45 Standard, showing just how much rare wood and hand-built craftsmanship increases the overall value of the instrument, as well as the price the consumer has to pay to have it.

Opposite page: a closer look at the Gibson J-45 Legend

Gibson

Hummingbird True Vintage

The boys in Bozeman strike again for Gibson, crafting another acoustic guitar in the tradition of its original. The Hummingbird in its vintage construction is a square shoulder dreadnought with a solid, premium Sitka spruce top and mahogany back and sides. The tone is rich and lilting, some would even say ruby-throated. A round mahogany neck with (Madagascar) rosewood fingerboard provides easy playability over mother of pearl parallelogram inlays.

Binding is 6-ply on top and 4-ply on the back. Vintage "Green Keys" tuners, a mother of pearl crown inlay on the headstock, tortoise "hummingbird" pickguard and a traditional Gibson rosewood bridge complete the look. Much of the materials that go into the Hummingbird are similar to that of the J-45 Legend, which is indicative of the luthier's attention to detail for woods and other materials which would have been used in the original instrument's creation in the 1940s.

Opposite page: Dave Murray
performing live onstage, playing
Gibson Hummingbird acoustic

Gibson's American Beginnings

The company that would become the industry leader in quality guitar craftsmanship began humbly in the 1890s, founded by Orville Gibson in Kalamazoo, Michigan. There he invented the archtop guitar in a one-man workshop, and worked tirelessly in the attempt to meet the increasing demand for his instruments. Eventually unable to do so, Gibson sold his business to a group of music store owners and attorneys.

Gibson had begun producing mainly mandolins, which were the more popular instrument at the time, but by the end of the 1920's it was clear the guitar was on the rise and would not be denied its place in music history. Gibson's archtop models were the best selling in their field and in 1926 conceded the guitar its place and created the L-1, its first flat-top, though from the look of the original guitar, it was apparent that Gibson still was not convinced that the instrument was for more serious musicians.

Still, they were popular, and selling. With the rise of other companies like the young and fiscally scrappy Epiphone, Gibson pushed the production of its archtop models to be bigger and louder than that of the competition. The same year, the company also released a more serious attempt at a flat-top acoustic guitar, the round-shouldered Jumbo. Gibson's competition with Epiphone, (in this case) lead to the development of their foundation instruments (The Super Jumbo, L-0, and L-00) for blues players of that time period, as well as laying the groundwork for lines that would lead to the creation of the J-45 and the Hummingbird.

What Gibson calls their "polite rivalry" with Epiphone would continue until Gibsons's purchase of the company in 1957. The company maintains domestic production facilities in Nasvhille, Tennessee (where the original plant in Kalamazoo ended up in 1971) and Bozeman, Montana, where luthiers keep up the tradition of crafting fine mandolins that were the company's initial instrument of choice.

Gibson

1937 L-00 Legend

A landmark Release for the Acoustic Guitar

This acoustic guitar is a painstaking reissue of the original instrument produced by Gibson in the late 1930s. This release is based on musician Lee Roy Parnell's original 1937 L-00. Ironic of course, is that the company that so famously made the originals neglected to keep one for themselves, just in case.

Gibson's 1937 L-00 acoustic features period-accurate white button tuners that are custom made for this guitar using the exact dimensions and design as were used on the original 1937 model. Each one is reproduced with precise handcrafted detail, ensuring the highest quality vintage tuner not available on any other instrument. As already evidenced, the luthiers at Gibson will go to any length to create an exact replica, even requesting a CAT scan.

Opposite page: a closer look at the Gibson 1937 L-00 Legend acoustic guitar

Putting the real thing in your hands

The fingerboard of Gibson's 1937 L-00 is constructed from the highest grade Madagascar rosewood available, which is personally inspected and qualified by Gibson's team of skilled experts before it enters the Gibson factories. The resilience of this durable wood makes the fingerboard extremely balanced and stable, and gives each chord and note unique clarity and singular attack. The L-00's vintage dot inlays are made from mother of pearl, and are inserted into the fingerboard using a process that eliminates gaps and doesn't require the use of fillers (synthetics that would not have been available in the 1930s). The fingerboard also sports traditional binding over the fret ends, which was a staple feature of many classic Gibson acoustics for many years.

True to form, the 1937 L-00's top is made from Adirondack Red Spruce, while the back and sides are constructed from Honduran mahogany, giving the 1937 L-00 a combination of tonewoods and features that produce a volume and clarity that was the hallmark of its popularity at its original production run. It evokes the rich, warm tone central to the traditional blues tones of the early 1900s. Selecting the right wood, as well as the formula to dry it out, are two of the most central procedures to Gibson's guitar-building process. Beginning with its first catalog in 1903, Gibson has assured its customers that every guitar would be built using woods with "the most durable, elastic, and sonorous qualities," and today's guitars from Gibson Acoustic are no different.

How Many Reissues Are Out There?

Vintage instruments and reissues bring back the undeniable look and feel of a bygone period in music and connect musicians to their musical pasts. They are testaments to a guitar company's long history of success and attention to craftsmanship. Gibson is just one of many companies to produce instruments that are faithful to their original creations as they (like others) have no doubt noticed that guitar players are willing to shell out big bucks for something well made and connected to musical glory. Inspiration in music may come from anywhere, but playing a guitar that is exactly like the one Robert Johnson or Bo Diddley may have played certainly helps the process.

Gibson

J-200 Custom

Originally built to be the flagship instrument for its flat-top line of acoustic guitars, the Jumbo-200 was introduced as a custom instrument for country singer/cowboy Ray Whitley in 1937. It was built in their workshop in Kalamazoo, Michigan. The Jumbo was named for its super large 16 7/8" flat top body, with a double-braced red spruce top and rosewood back and sides and sunburst finish. The layout of the guitar changed in 1947, when the name changed to the J-200, with maple back and sides. Gibson changed the name again for the last time to the SJ-200 by the 1950s.

Due to the weak post-depression economy and wartime belt-tightening, demand for this high end guitar was very limited and production quantities were small. Early models made from rosewood are highly prized by collectors as it is largely unavailable in quantities large enough to produce an entire instrument anymore.

The King of the Flat-Tops

This updated model of the original J-200 (built by Gibson's acoustic division in Bozeman, MT) is equipped with the revolutionary Fishman Aura Ellipse system, and the J-200 Custom allows acoustic musicians to easily and precisely reproduce the sound of an acoustic guitar as if it had been enhanced with a microphone in a professional studio. The Fishman Aura Ellipse system was programmed to reproduce studio sounds with Class A microphone preamplifiers and a mix of vintage and modern microphones to create Aura Acoustic images that complement the specific tone qualities of the J-200 Custom. In short, the guitar has been built to sound exactly the same when plugged into an amp as it does standing alone. It's a rare achievement for any acoustic guitar to boast of, as the main complaint of amplified instruments was their lack of ability to maintain the same deep resonance and tonality when plugged in.

The make-up of the J-200 is very similar to Gibson's other reissue (or recreation) models in their use of similar woods and accessories. Ebony for its fingerboard, graduated crown in-lays are made from mother of pearl, a dovetail neck joint, and similar hand-scalloped bracing is used inside the body as with other hand-crafted Gibson acoustics. Indian rosewood is used for the back and sides (reflected in its price) of the J-200 Custom. Rosewood was used in the original series of guitars Gibson produced only up until WWII, then maple was used, and, because of the guitar's price tag at that time, it became something of a status symbol for Grand Ole Opry invitees and C&W performers around the United States.

Wartime marked the shift in dominance from the arch-top guitar to the flat-top style of guitar which Gibson had already begun (if somewhat begrudgingly) to transition into. Gibson was purchased by the behemoth Chicago Musical Instruments Corporation in 1944, though unlike CBS' buy-out of Fender, CMI did little to hault or creatively stunt the directions of Gibson and, if anything, buoyed the company through the lean years of war that spanned the globe. Still, even in wartime, Gibson continued a production schedule that, while sparse, continued to produce genre defining instruments.

Left: J-200 Custom.
Opposite page: Cliff Richard, performing live onstage, playing Gibson J200 acoustic guitar

Gibson

Robert Johnson L-1

Legend, myth, icon, Delta blues man to end all, Robert Johnson recorded sparingly - his life and death shrouded in mystery, and his music poured and puzzled over for generations. There has also been much discussion of his playing techniques, and even the tunings he used to make those landmark recordings. Only two photos exist of Robert Johnson, and one shows the musician holding his trademark instrument, the Gibson L-1. Johnson is regarded by many musicians as the grandfather of rock & roll, due to his infectious influence on many musicians the likes of Bob Dylan, Eric Clapton, Jeff Beck, and Led Zeppelin.

It is only fitting that the man whose hauntingly complex sound inspired so many have an instrument named after him - the special signature edition Gibson Robert Johnson L-1 Acoustic Guitar. Everything about this acoustic guitar has been expertly re-created, from the shallow L-1 body design to the 25" scale. The authentic ebony bridge has the original, beautifully carved pyramid wings and the soundhole diameter remains at 3-3/4". Even period-correct hardware is used. The only modern refinement to the design is the tasteful inclusion of Robert Johnson's signature inlaid with mother-of-pearl in the fingerboard.

Deals with the Devil and Quick Recordings

Many tales surround the legendary playing ability of Robert Johnson. One such myth involves his meeting with Old Scratch himself at the Crossroads (hence 'Crossroad Blues') of a local Mississippi Plantation. There he met the Devil, who tuned his L-1 guitar. When he returned it to Johnson, the blues man had gained mastery over the instrument, but with a price. Nothing is known of Johnson's early life, and records discovered over time point to different dates for his birth.

His death occurred in the same location where his infernal powers had been given him - the crossroads. There are even a number of accounts and theories as to how Johnson died or was killed. Some say it was poison, sudden illness, or perhaps the Devil returning to collect his due. There are currently three grave sites that claim to be the final resting place of Johnson, all lying in and around the town of Greenwood, Mississippi where he died.

Johnson's recording sessions were sparse, all occurring during 1936-1937, in and out of hotel rooms and small studios. One track, "Hellhound on My Tail," (recorded in Texas) fleshes out a popular theme for Johnson and his short run of music: fear of the devil. Other themes in Johnson's music include impotence ("Dead Shrimp Blues" and "Phonograph Blues") and infidelity ("Terraplane Blues," "If I Had Possession Over Judgement Day" and "Love in Vain"). Six of Johnson's blues songs mention the devil or some form of the supernatural.

In "Me And The Devil" he began, "Early this morning when you knocked upon my door/Early this morning…when you knocked upon my door/And I said, 'Hello, Satan, I believe it's time to go,'" before leading into "You may bury my body down by the highway side/You may bury my body, down by the highway side/So my old evil spirit can catch a Greyhound bus and ride."

Opposite page: Robert Johnson L-1 acoustic guitar Left: Kurt Wagner performing on stage with a Gibson acoustic guitar.

Gibson

Songmaker Dreadnought Solid Mahogany

Gibson's DSM Dreadnought guitar from the Songmaker series features a J-45 headstock, the rosette of the SJ-200, the pickguard from the Blues King, and the bridge from the Woody Guthrie Southern Jumbo. Gibson blended these vintage features with two classic body styles: the foundational dreadnought and the grand concert, and traditional guitar-making woods including mahogany and rosewood. Part Frankenstein (not the Eddie Van Halen variety), part intricate recipe, the Songmaker shows off the versatility of Gibson's luthiers.

These Gibson guitars are all made from solid wood and incorporate features such as Gibson's traditional scalloped bracing, double acting truss rods, and premium Sitka spruce tops. Other significant appointments include a solid mahogany, 25-1/2-inch scale neck with an ebony fingerboard, rosewood or white boltaron binding, genuine mother of pearl dot inlays, chrome hardware, and Tusq saddles, nuts, and bridge pins. The headstock and peghead carry the Gibson logo in silk-screened gold letters.

This superior performance model has built-in active Fishman electronics, with an undersaddle pickup/miniature electret microphone and preamp combination. Blend the pickup and microphone together for a powerful and cohesive acoustic guitar tone that is deeper and more "filled out", than the sound of either the microphone or pickup alone. Levels are set by the master volume and blend controls. Traditional shelving-style bass and treble, plus a semi-parametric "Contour" EQ are included so you can shape your guitar's tone exactly to taste.

The Tireless Work of Master Luthiers

Gibson's Bozeman Team of luthiers has slowly but surely reintroduced the company's line of vintage instruments in a way that is true to their original design and accessible for the modern acoustic guitar player. Gibson has since broken up the acoustic guitar division into several "production lines." True Vintage encompasses accurate renditions of past models, the J-45 being a prime example; Modern Classics includes guitars that adapt these templates to the varied needs of modern performers; the Legends Series includes dead-on, period-correct reproductions of highly prized original instruments such as the Robert Johnson L-1, and the Signature Artist Series offers renditions based on the specific guitars-or guitars tailored toward the needs of several major artists (some are shown here). In addition, the Songmaker Series includes high-quality but back-to-basics models designed to suit the needs of contemporary singer-songwriters - the DSM being a prime example. Taken as a comprehensive range, the entire output represents the best acoustic guitars Gibson has made in some 50 or 60 years.

It is all due to the craftsman and their tireless attention to detail. Throughout the history of the acoustic guitar or stringed instruments in general, whether it be with Fender, Alvarez, Gibson, or any other company, each guitar's strength is always determined at the outset from the ability of its luthiers, the ground level designers of the instruments that the company then brings into the world on a larger scale. Without these artists, their tools, and the fine woods used in creating guitars, there would be no instrument for a musician to pick up. For that, we say thank you.

Opposite page and below: Gibson DSM from the Songmaker series

Elvis Presley Dove

No history is complete without a mention of its King. Elvis Presley brought the Blues to American homes in a way that has never been duplicated. In a career that experienced many highs, lows, down-and-outs, and comeback triumphs, Presley remained the consummate performer and sometimes underrated musician. Some of the most enduring images of Elvis Presley are on stage during his Las Vegas run of performances in the 1970's. A fair majority of the pictures of those performances show the King of Rock and Roll holding one of the most celebrated, if not recognizable, acoustic guitars in the world—a custom 1969 Gibson Dove with an ebony finish. Gibson pays tribute to that guitar with the Elvis Presley Dove Signature Artist Series acoustic, a carefully crafted replica of Elvis' famed guitar that includes many of the same features as his original.

The guitar is built in the Dove's dreadnought body style and features a truss rod cover engraved with Elvis' signature. Super-flash looks come from gloss ebony finish, split parallelogram mother-of-pearl fretboard inlays, rosewood bridge, checkerboard marquetry, and multi-ply binding. Loud, high-integrity tone comes from a solid Sitka spruce top and solid curly maple back and sides, round profile curly maple neck and 25-3/4" scale and nickel Grover tuners.

Elvis Presley the Musical Icon

If Robert Johnson was the technical architect of the blues and the grandfather of rock & roll, Elvis was the frontman, consummate in his mastery of a crowd and manipulation of the media. Never before him had an artist so infused himself into the fabric of American consciousness - from his forbidden hips, to his service in the military, to movie fame and sold out arenas world wide, Elvis was the first multimedia icon. He generated so much star power that his fans would not let him rest even in death. Entire cultures have cropped up around Elvis impersonation, and even now, when the King would probably have been dead from natural causes, there are those who still cling to the notion that their beloved idol has not yet left the building.

The Las Vegas Years

Elvis first performed in Las Vegas in 1956 when he was a young man, just 21 years old. He was booked in the Venus Room at the New Frontier hotel, billed as "The Atomic Powered Singer" (presumably because of those previously mentioned hips).

While he was already becoming quite popular with teens around the country, Elvis was not the typical Las Vegas Strip entertainer of the time, and his shows were met with a sense of cool disinterest. Despite Elvis' less than warm reputation with the burning city in the desert, it was not until the International Hotel opened in 1969, that Elvis truly became synonymous with Las Vegas.

In 1969 Elvis performed his first show at the International to a sold-out crowd, and went on to perform regular engagements at the property for seven years – a total of 837 consecutive sold-out performances in front of 2.5 million people. The sheer numbers from these performances are staggering. In one 29-day period Elvis entertained 101,509 guests, bringing in $1.5 million in ticket sales. In the course of his 800-plus performances in Vegas, Elvis sold $43.7 million in show tickets, about $250 million in 2007 dollars. In the months when Elvis was performing (according to the city of Las Vegas), one of every two visitors to the city saw Elvis's show!

Opposite page: circa 1975: American rock singer Elvis Presley (1935 - 1977), wearing a white rhinestone-studded suit and strapped Gibson Dove

Gibson

J-185 EC Rosewood

This acoustic guitar represents Gibson's most recent interpretation of its Jumbo line as an electric hybrid. The Gibson J-185 EC Rosewood Acoustic Electric Guitar's comfortable jumbo cutaway body style combines the best of playability and clear gilded notes, represented in deft fashion by the Fishman Prefix Plus-T pickup system with built-in tuner. Solid premium Sitka spruce top on solid Indian rosewood back and sides produce wonderful resonance with tonal integrity. Brilliant visual appointments include 4-ply top binding, bound back, bound ebony fingerboard, and gold Grover tuners.

Gibson put the first crown peghead logo on an ES-300 back in 1940, and it has graced the headstocks of many legendary Gibson guitars ever since, including the J-185 EC. Since that time it has also been called a "thistle" because of its resemblance to the group of flowering plants with the sharp prickles, though Gibson has preferred to call it a "crown."

The J-185 also represents one of the more affordable American-made Gibsons on the market today. With artist renditions like the Robert Johnson and the Elvis Presley clocking in at two to three times the cost of the J-185, its clear why an aspiring guitar player would turn to this Jumbo for some musical comfort. There is no slacking in material quality with the J-185, as it is still composed of tried and true woods like rose and mahogany. Like all other Gibson acoustics, it has been built by the Gibson Acoustic Workshop in Bozeman, Montana.

Opposite page: Pete Doherty performs on stage with his Gibson guitar

The Progression of the Jumbo Acoustic

As a company, Gibson has continued to improve upon the well crafted originals that are its founding for success. What began with the SJ-200 in 1937 has now been carefully and artfully marched forward with the J-185, an acoustic model that reveals the technological advances in amplification without sacrificing wood quality or the need to ship production to an off-shore site where craftsmanship will be at less than an artisan level. Where other companies seem to give in to the lure of cheaper production costs and higher ranges in profit, Gibson seems to balk. That is not to say that they have shunned the quick and dirty factory world all together. Epiphone has produced less expensive models of the Gibson made classics since its purchase in the early part of the 1950s but has still been permitted its signature, luthier driven projects.

The jumbo acoustic as a body style has been one that has been very good to Gibson financially. Artists like Elvis Costello have brought great fame to the once degraded flat-top instrument that Gibson only started pushing to compete with rival guitar companies. The body type investment has proven to be a smart move from a company that has rarely made a misstep when it comes to providing the best equipment available. That their instruments bare the price tag they do is yet another sign of the cost of finer goods in the face of dwindling supply.

Gibson

Woody Guthrie SJ

When he penned "This Land is Your Land" in the 1940s, Woody Guthrie cemented himself as a songwriter and as a true piece of American history. Woody Guthrie's 1945 Southern Jumbo has been recreated by Gibson in honor of that occasion, and keeps with it the many nuances of the original. No mere toy, this acoustic guitar is constructed from the finest woods in the arsenal of the Gibson's craftsman in an attempt to produce a new guitar that is not unlike the original. A Sitka spruce top on select Honduran mahogany back and sides, 6-ply top binding and 4-ply back binding, V-shape neck profile, mother-of-pearl parallelogram fretboard inlays, and Fishman Matrix electronics all work to create an acoustic guitar with Gibson's latest technological flare, and with Guthrie's country aesthetic still in mind.

A visit from the family was what actually birthed the idea for this commemorative guitar. Woody's son Arlo (who has created his own musical legacy) visited Gibson in 2002, and the end result was the eventual creation of the replica we have available to the public.

The Jumbo Acoustic and the Super Jumbo

"The main confusion seems to lie in the fact that, on hearing the term "Jumbo," many players picture the seminal SJ-200," writes Gibson's Dave Hunter, "The groundbreaking curvaceous flat-top introduced in 1938, which had the largest body width of its day at 17" across its circular lower bout. Correctly speaking, however, this is the Super Jumbo, and was originally dubbed the Super Jumbo 200, later abbreviated to SJ-200. When first used all on its lonesome, the name "Jumbo" actually referred to a large-bodied, round-shouldered flat-top introduced a few years before, in 1934, which had echoed the shape of an even earlier model, Gibson's large HG Hawaiian guitar of 1929."

The gentlemen stationed at Gibsons' super-secret acoustic guitar compound in Bozeman have worked hard to clear up the confusion that the varying product line names have caused. Models on the Jumbo side of things (headed by the justifiably "Super" 200 model, now again called the SJ-200) have the distinctive circular lower bout and oval-shaped upper bout, while the very different models that mirror the more venerable "Jumbo" of the 1930s are classified as Round Shoulder Dreadnoughts (which further distinguishes them from a popular series of Square Shoulder Dreadnoughts). While this may clear the issues and holster the pistols of guitar players around the world, for the layperson, the nuances of the instruments may lay more within the sound than any actual physical representation of the instruments.

Gitane

D-500 Maccaferri Style Jazz Guitar

In the style of the original

Gitane Guitars produces replica/homage style instruments that are mock-ups of the original Macaferri/Selmer guitars favored by Django Reinhardt and other "hot club" Gypsy players of the 1930s. Guitars of this style were almost always too expensive for those without the start up capital to afford, but Gitane has provided a more economical model for the average acoustic guitar player.

Followers of Gypsy-Jazz guitar, as well as guitar purists of multiple traditions will applaud the re-introduction of the classic Selmer-Maccaferri style jazz guitar. The Gitane D-500 possesses all the measurements and characteristic features that the original models carried, but are produced using the latest technology so as to keep the price low (relatively speaking) and the affordability high. The Gitane D-500 is built from select solid spruce with rosewood back and sides and a thin, bound mahogany neck with a 24-fret extension fingerboard of ebony with pearl-dot position markers. The large D-shaped soundhole has concentric rings of multicolored wood purfling. The body is bound with solid ebony for durability and beauty with maple/walnut/maple purfling on all edges.

The History of Maccaferri and Selmer

The Selmer Guitar is an interesting and off-color acoustic guitar best known as the favored instrument of Django Rheinhardt, and was produced by Selmer from 1932 to about 1952. Before the advent of amplification, Selmers had the same kind of appeal for European players that the archtop guitar did in America: it was loud enough to be heard over the other instruments in a band. It was a common theme running through music at the outset of the 1930s, which is why the advent of amplification was so important for the instrument's continued health.

The "petite bouche" model has an especially loud and cutting voice, and even today it remains the design preferred by lead players in Django-style bands, while the accompanying rhythm players often use D-hole instruments (This was the lineup in Django's Quintette du Hot Club de France during its classic period in the late 1930s, and it remains the pattern for bands that emulate them). Modern proponents of the style amplify their instruments in concert, but may still play acoustically in small venues and jam sessions. Gypsy jazz players usually couple the guitar with light, silver-coated silk-and-steel strings and heavy tortoiseshell guitar picks. For this style, the look matters as much as the performance itself.

In more "recent times", the Selmer guitar is almost completely associated with Django Reinhardt and the "gypsy jazz" school of his followers. From the 1930s through to the 1950s, however, Selmers were used by all types of performers in France and (in the 1940s) in the United Kingdom.

The first Selmers sold to the UK market were used in the standard dance band context and associated with performers the likes of Al Bowlly. In France, the Selmer was the top professional guitar for many years and can be heard in everything from musette (a style of dance popular in the 1800s in France) to the backing of chansonniers (a vocal-centric French song). Leading players ranged from Henri Crolla to Sascha Distel.

Gitane

DG-255 Selmer-Maccaferri Style Jazz Guitar

The Gitane DG-255 Selmer-Maccaferri Style Jazz Guitar carries a tone from a different time. The super-wide bridge, oval soundhole (signifying it as a lead instrument, "petite bouche"), and slotted head have a more modern appearance but were actually all found on Django Reinhardt's guitar of the 1930s.

Its large top with light bracing made possible by the long bridge was loud enough to be heard unamplified with his Quintet of the Hot Club of France. Select solid spruce top, longer scale length, and rosewood back and sides produce resonant, bright attack. Ebony body binding with triple maple/walnut purfling, mahogany neck with ebony fretboard, bone nut with zero fret, compensated moveable center on the bridge, nickel-plated open-geared tuners, adjustable truss rod, and trapeze tailpiece combine to make this a piece of jazz history that has been reinterpreted for the modern audience and musician seeking a link to the where their style has evolved from.

Why is the Past so Important?

The 1930s saw the need for greater volume than typical flat top guitars provided. In the US, makers responded with the punchy oval and then F hole archtop models, resonator guitars, and increasingly large flat tops. In Europe, classical guitarist and Italian-trained luthier Mario Maccaferri designed guitars for the Selmer Company of Paris, France and produced a beautiful instrument with a large D shaped hole – the Orchestra or "grande bouche" model acoustic guitar.

This guitar has twelve frets to the body, and originally hosted an internal resonator, though that was quickly abandoned. The grande bouche remained in production from 1932 to 1934, when a contract dispute drove Maccaferri and Selmer apart. The Gitane D-500 copies this original nicely but for a more modest price. Following the breakup, Selmer developed the 14-fret "Modele Jazz" or "petite bouche" guitar with a small oval vertical soundhole. The Gitane DG-255 is a reproduction of this guitar. The other Gitane models are derived from the basic platform, but vary.

While Django Reinhardt played a Selmer guitar and later picked up a US made archtop, Maccaferri himself probably remained unfamiliar with Reinhardt and his music. Reinhardt's oval holed petite bouche model, Selmer guitar #503, currently rests in the Conservatoire Nationale in Paris.

Mario Maccaferri was a classical guitarist, and designed his Concert Model with fan bracing for use with gut strings. The bridge is glued on, and the neck is relatively wide, but because of the easily flexed top, big top size, and cutaway, it is also a wonderful instrument for classical, Brazilian, and jazz. Unfortunately, a relatively inexpensive reproduction is not available. The DG-255 is the least costly instrument produced by Gitane at this time and still bears the weight of expense for the emerging guitar player.

These facts bear significance for the modern acoustic guitar player who is deciding where their sound rests, and what style best suits the way in which they choose to approach the instrument. The history of an instrument helps the guitarist to learn the original intent or reason for its creation, and as such, what style best allows the instrument to shine.

Godin

Multiac Steel Duet

Godin Guitars sits just outside the United States in Quebec, Canada. The company started producing guitars designed by Robert Godin (namesake and owner) in 1982, and since that time have garnered an industry reputation as being an innovator with traditional roots, winning several awards for their proprietarily modern acoustic guitar models. The Multiac series of acoustic guitars have been constructed in both steel and nylon string models. Here, the Steel Duet is examined.

Outwardly, the Steel and Nylon models look very similar, while inside lies a tale of two different constructions. The top of the Steel string Multiac incorporates a modern variation on the classic X-brace. The slim necks and shallow bodies of these guitars make them exceptionally comfortable to play, and coupled with the X-bracing allow them to handle the increased tension/resonance without bowing. The two-chamber body design (mahogany for the body and spruce for the top) resists feedback and the custom voiced preamps make for great performance sound performance with minimal effort.

The Mission and the Architects

Godin guitars are manufactured at one of six factories in either Canada or the United States.

"…why not just have one giant guitar factory?" writes Godin, "although there are some obvious inconveniences associated with spreading ourselves out this much, the up-side is that these smaller operations promote a more intimate working environment which gets everybody more involved and this is reflected in the instruments themselves." Godin guitars are assembled at the company's Richmond, Quebec, Berlin, and New Hampshire factories. All necks and bodies are built at their original location in La Patrie, Quebec.

What is significant about Godin's construction methods is their desire to keep their workshops on shore. It allows for greater oversight in the production process and a stronger adherence to the original intent of the guitar's designer, usually founder Robert Godin. From the company's beginning, they have divided these factories between their acoustic and electric guitar lines and say that the company began their electric factories as part suppliers (mostly necks) for other guitar companies. "You might be amazed to find out how many different guitar brands are all being produced in the same handful of factories," writes Godin Guitars, "we're not telling you this because we want to divulge somebody's secrets but simply to let you know where we're coming from." This time spent producing guitar parts for other companies allowed Godin to see the dimensions future competitors were working with, and he then used that knowledge to incorporate his own innovations into the designs that are now their current run of acoustic and electric guitars.

Godin believes that the guitar is a fashion statement. They do not back away from this ethos for one moment, constructing instruments that are at once eye-catching and structurally sound. Indeed, Godin has continued to delve further into the conceptual mind of guitar creation, building unique instruments such as the Glissentar - an eleven string, fretless, acoustic/electric guitar. With such innovations rolling out, it is exciting to see what Robert Godin and his team will do next.

*Above: A closer look at the
Godin Multiac Steel Duet*

Godin

Multiac Grand Concert Duet Ambience

The Multiac Grand Concert Duet Ambiance is from Godin's nylon string camp, and features the latest technology in their custom electronics by Fishman (the same company supplying Gibson with the electronics for their acoustic/electrics). This allows the player to select between 4 individual mic settings. Each guitarist may choose between these blendable sound imaging microphones via the 4-way selector switch which includes Treble, Mid, and Bass as well as a Phase button and Blend slider. Much like other Multiac Grand Concert models, the guitar's design unites a larger body with a solid cedar top, and a neck that joins the body at the twelfth fret. The 2" width at the nut is slightly larger than the standard Multiac and more typical of the classical tradition.

Like a classical guitar, the fingerboard has no inlays whatsoever, but it does come with side dot markers on the 3rd, 5th, 7th and 12th frets for those players that would still require a little fingerboard life rafting. Following its Multiac siblings, all of the controls are placed in the same location as a Gibson Les Paul toggle switch, but the similarities end there. The Grand Concert is built from similar woods as other Godin models: chambered mahogany for its body, an ebony fingerboard, and solid cedar for the top.

The Guitar as a Piece of Art

Godin has time and again addressed the versatility of the guitar as both an instrument and a means by which an artist (the luthier) expresses the true beauty in their craft. "Unlike many other instruments that follow a fairly strict set of design parameters," writes Godin Guitars, "such as most orchestral instruments, guitars truly lend themselves to variation in design. This capacity for variation manifests itself in two distinct ways, there is the purely visual variation such as, the lightning-bolt-shaped-pointy-headstock-you're-obviously-not-in-an-easy-listening-band guitar… Don't get us wrong, we are committed to high aesthetic values in all of our designs but what we find most compelling is the other type of variation inspired by the endless musical possibilities in guitar design." Godin has continued their experimentation with even the most basic of guitar edicts, such as the location of an acoustic guitar's soundhole, traditionally placed beneath the strings at the base of the instrument. The luthiers at Godin have upended this concept altogether and with the aid of modern technology (pickups and preamps), created a look for their instruments that is both aesthetically appealing and musically progressive.

The Summer of 2009 marks the fifth edition of the ever popular Montreal Musical Instrument Show, also known as the SIMM, presented from July 10th - 12th as part of the 30th annual Festival International de Jazz de Montréal. Montreal based Godin Guitars is once again a proud sponsor and has returned to collaborate with SIMM and Jazz Fest organizers in order to help make this year's silent auction a success. Godin produced five custom models for the Festival's auction in collaboration with Robert Godin and artist-in-residence Yves Archambault. These creative masterpieces have also all been given individual names by the artist, such as "Pythagoras", "Dublin", "Peace", "Black Zebra" and "Orpheus" respectively.

Opposite Page: a closer look at the Multiac Grand Concert Ambience

G400 Synchromatic

This acoustic guitar produced by Gretsch is crafted from selected rock maple for its back, sides and neck, has a fine-grained spruce top, and is finished in hand polished dark brown lacquer with sunburst shadings. The Synchromatic revitalizes the make of the archtop guitar for a newer generation. The edges of the body, fingerboard, headpiece and guard plate are fully bound in extra wide black and ivory celluloid. Other fittings include the easy playing, steel-reinforced neck, oval rosewood fingerboard with extra broad nickel silver frets, "Chromatic" tailpiece and "Synchronized" bridge.

The Chromatic Tailpiece

The Synchromatic 400 "Chromatic Tailpiece" is an exclusive Gretsch feature. The tailpiece is designed to compensate for differing string gauges, thereby reducing tension and equalizing playing finger pressure. The tailpiece makes playing easier with uniform finger action. What this allows for is versatility - the acoustic guitar player shouldering a guitar equipped with a chromatic tailpiece, like the G400, has complete control over how heavy or light the guitar will sound.

A Tale of Four Freds

Friedrich Gretsch founded the company that bears his name in Brooklyn in 1883. By 1895 the founder of the burgeoning guitar workshop had died, leaving the business to his son, Fred Gretsch. As a young man, Fred Jr. took what his father had created and built it into the popular guitar company that would take over a ten story building on Broadway twenty years later. Acoustic guitars were the best sellers for Gretsch in their early days (before the advent of electronics) and Fred then left his company to his son in 1942 when the Gretsch "sound" was incredibly strong. Three Freds down, one to go. While Fred III. served his country in the Navy, the company was managed by his brother Bill. Rock & Roll was quite successful for the Gretsch family, and in 1967 the company was purchased by music industry giant Baldwin.

Gretsch remained the property of Baldwin for almost twenty years until 1985, when a determined Fred W. Gretsch bought back his great-grandfather's company to return it once again to family hands. That makes four Freds. The production center for Gretsch Guitars has since moved to Savannah, Georgia, where guitar, as well as drum production, continues to this day.

The Workshop versus the Corporation

"Family owned" is often a phrase bandied about by many corporations in order to legitimize their roots within a specific community, or to link their heritage to humble beginnings. We have seen throughout the history, craft and production of the guitar, that larger companies, and mogul-style corporations have often become poor stewards of the once small businesses and workshops that they have taken over. Production and quality slipped to all but nothing when Fender was bought by CBS, Gibson barely survived a buyout form CMI in 1944, and Epiphone is possibly the lone successful company to be acquired and thrive without suffering a period of low production. What keeps the acoustic guitar relevant in music, songwriting and art is passion. It must be handled by those that have a true love for its creation and not simply the bottom line of its profitability in mind.

Gretsch

Synchromatic Cutaway Filter'Tron

It is the Cat's Eye. The G6040MCSS is a customized version of the original 400C Synchromatic, with the addition of a single "High Sensitive" Filter'Tron pickup in the neck position. With its select curly maple body and fine-grained spruce top, the G6040MCSS Synchromatic Cutaway is a look back though Gretsch's rich history of guitar production. The edges of the body, fingerboard, headstock and pickguard are fully bound in extra wide black and ivory celluloid. Other fittings include the easy to play oval rosewood fingerboard with extra broad nickel silver frets. A Chromatic tailpiece and Synchronized bridge are also worked in.

Unique features for the Synchromatic Acoustic include inlaid Pearloid Split Hump Block Position Markers, Black Headstock Overlay, Pearloid Headstock Inlay, Bound Fingerboard, Multiple Body Bindings, "Cat's-Eye" Sound-Holes, Bound Tortoise Shell Streamlined Pickguard, Knurled Strap Retainer Knobs, and an adjustable Truss Rod.

What is the Filter'Tron?

The Filter'Tron "Electronic Guitar Head" was introduced in 1957 at the summer NAMM (National Association of Music Merchants) show in Chicago. Filter'Tron pickups feature dual-coils and are designed to filter out the electronic hum normally associated with single-coil pickups, while adding a warmer tone, and a significant increase in output and sustain. Its application in an acoustic guitar is a bit incongruous to what has been the industry standard in acoustic guitar design for many years. This guitar is an acoustic only in the strictest sense of word, as its outward appearance from a distance would suggest it to be totally electrified (as the pickup is more used for electric guitars) and lack a hollow body all together. The acoustic appeal of the instrument appears as an accessory to the hardware's innate power, which is an interesting innovation from Gretsch, as it incorporates their traditional strengths in electronic production with the sustaining resonance of the acoustic guitar.

The NAMM Show

The acronym NAMM originally stood for the National Association of Music Merchants, but has evolved from a national entity representing the interests of music products retailers, to an international association including both commercial, retail members and affiliates. The long form of the name is no longer used, as it no longer truly represents the intent of the organization, and now it is simply known as NAMM (the International Music Products Association). The group has worked to create initiatives for music in inner cities and with urban youth, and created scholarship and grant funding in a continuing effort to create music lovers and producers of all ages.

The NAMM Foundation is a non-profit organization with the mission of advancing active participation in music making across the lifespan by supporting scientific research, philanthropic giving and public service programs from the international music products industry. For NAMM, music's greatest product is the people that create it. "Industry support of NAMM's tradeshows allows the NAMM Board to give back to these worthy programs," says Joe Lamond, president and CEO of NAMM. "The grants will help to create more music makers and the scholarships will help to recruit the best and brightest who will become the future leaders of the industry."

Gretsch

G6022 Rancher

Built in the style pioneered by the Gibson J-200, The Gretsch Rancher hits the scales at 17" wide, 3-1/2" to 4-1/2" deep, with maple back and sides and a spruce top. It has multiple bindings on the body, headpiece and neck and a patented French design sound hole. The neck is laminated rock maple; the fingerboard is bound rosewood. The western motif pearl inlays hint at the instrument's wide-open, big sound. The Rancher acoustic is complete with gold plated hardware, enclosed gear machines, acoustic-design pin-bridge and Western maple stain finish.

This model is based on the original model produced by Gretsch in the early part of the 20th century and as such features no electronics. Even so, the Rancher and its more subtle partner, the Town & Country, never caught fire with players like Gretsch's electrics have done over the years. For some players, the Rancher sounds thin, which creates an odd contrast to the guitar's Jumbo style frame. Others may have avoided it in favor of more traditional acoustics from Martin or Gibson. For whatever reason, Gretsch's flagship acoustic has rarely received the attention that other guitar companies have garnered, even though famous guitar players of the period such as Gene Vincent were often seen playing one. As we can see, The Rancher is still being produced, but the Town & Country has not seen the light of day since 1957.

Gretsch and Fender Partnership

Fast Forward to 2002, when Fender and Gretsch reached an agreement giving the California based guitar giant principal control over the marketing, production, and distribution of Gretsch's instruments. Fender quickly set about improving the line by upgrading substandard electrical components and bringing modern production more closely in line with designs and practices of the classic era. Body and headstock shapes, which on reissues from the 90s and early 2000s had varied from 50s-60s practices, were made more vintage correct. Classic never goes out of style, that is why they're called classics.

Hollowbodies were returned to 3-ply construction rather than the 5-plies of the 1990-2002 period of design. Filtertron double-coil pickups were redesigned by TV Jones to sound more like vintage pickups. Duo Jets were more extensively chambered, again in accordance with vintage practice, and the trestle bracing of the 1959-1961 era was reintroduced on the Brian Setzer line and other selected models. All of this in an effort to give Gretsch the look that had traditionally been its strength, and more importantly, to give the players what they wanted.

An array of models based on vintage designs have been introduced, with widespread approval among players and even (to the surprise of some) collectors. While such judgments are always subjective and sometimes contentious, many feel FMIC-era (the time period after their partnership came into effect) was when Gretsch guitars exhibited the highest level of overall build quality, attention to detail, and consistency in Gretsch's long history. The Rancher's current production quality is a testament to the relationship bearing positive fruit. This is a great example of a guitar company which understands the market and need for quality craftsmanship, steering the ship correctly and with passion.

Gretsch has also introduced new models consistent with their heritage, but aimed at modern players, with features like premium pickups designed by TV Jones, locking Sperzel tuners, and ML bracing designed by Mike Lewis of FMIC and Masao Terada of the Terada company in Japan, where all Gretsch pro-line guitars are now built. The Gretsch family still retains full ownership of Gretsch Guitars.

Opposite page: Jack White from The Raconteurs and White Stripes on his Gretsch acoustic guitar

Rancher Acoustic/Electric

The features of this electrified model of Grestch's acoustic Rancher include an exclusive Fishman Prefix Pro Pickup and Peamp, and Grover Sta-Tite machine head to compliment the Jumbo body style. Whereas players have complained about the Rancher's lack of punch and swell of sound, this model has a bit more oomph. This is due largely to Fishman, who has become the industry standard for acoustic electronics, and shows Fender's desire to keep Gretsch competing with the larger guitar companies, like the two-headed monster of Epiphone and Gibson.

Grestch and Chet Atkins

For Gretsch, there would be no better spokesman than Chet Atkins. Convinced by an extensive courtship, Atkins shouldered the Gretsch 6120, a model designed specially for him before he'd even accepted the invitation to play it - Gretsch took the risk and it paid off for them.

It was 1955, and the 6120 would go on to become the company's defining guitar, and Atkins their signature guitar virtuoso, a country artist with homegrown roots and national appeal. The 6120 would eventually be seen in the hands of The Who's Pete Townshend, and the journeyman Neil Young. Atkins would pass away in 2001, leaving a wealth of musical history and new musicians to hold onto his playing techniques and tailor-made hardware.

In January 2007, after reaching an agreement with the Atkins family, Gretsch announced the return of Chet Atkins as an endorser. The Country Classic models became Country Gentlemen. Once again, the name "Chet Atkins Hollowbody" returned to the 6120 Nashville Series, and the Tennessee Rose became the "Chet Atkins Tennessee Rose". In July 2008, a limited run of Chet Atkins 6120 Stereo guitars was introduced, based on a famous prototype from 1956 that had been featured in several landmark Atkins recordings, but were never produced in series.

What This Means for the Acoustic

What's good for the goose is usually good for the gander. This is no less true of Gretsch's success in the electric guitar market as it applies to the acoustic guitar end of their production. When a company has the services of a guitar legend like Chet Atkins, it lends credibility to their entire run of musical instruments. This in turn leads to increased sales and the ability to continue offering well crafted guitars. While not viewed as a principal strength of Gretsch's, the acoustic guitar is what founded the company so many years ago, and what sustained it as the electric guitar was still in its infancy and widely unreliable.

The Rancher is a versatile line for Gretsch, one that has seen many musicians pick it up and give it a try. What has yet to appear from the Fender/Gretsch partnership is the bleeding through of design aspects - that is, a representative high quality acoustic that bares the mark of Fender's luthiers, but with Gretsch's unmistakable body style and vintage flare. Perhaps it is Fender's intent to lead with the strongest foot, and to work with what the consumer is most excited about.

Opposite page: Bryan Adams
performing on stage, playing
Gretsch 6120 Chet Atkins guitar

Gretsch

Rancher Falcon Cutaway

This is a "White Falcon"-esque version of the Rancher that carries the same dimensions as the stock Gretsch Rancher: 17" wide, 3-1/2" to 4-1/2" deep, with maple for its back and sides, as well as spruce for the acoustic's top. It has multiple binding on the body, headpiece and neck, and a patented French design sound hole. The neck is laminated rock maple; the fingerboard is bound rosewood. The western motif is similar to that of other Rancher models but stands out in stark contrast with its white finish and well advanced electronics. The Rancher acoustic is complete with gold plated hardware, enclosed gear machines, acoustic-design pin-bridge and western maple stain finish. Gold Sparkle Bound Fingerboard, Multiple Body Bindings, Patented French Triangular Sound-Hole Design, Gold Plexi Pickguard with Falcon Motif, Knurled Strap Retainer Knobs, Adjustable Truss Rod are also series features that are included on the Falcon Cutaway.

Electronics on the Falcon include the Fishman Acoustic Matrix under the saddle pickup as well as a miniature electret condenser microphone mounted on the underside of the preamp chassis. The modern amenities are buoyed by time honored X-brace construction and a longer than average neck length, one that is more in line with an electric guitar at 21 frets. The jumbo body cutaway will allow greater player access to that extended neck.

The Gretsch Foundation and Guitar Art

In 2002 the Gretsch Company started an art program, where instruments were donated to schools and organizations to help them with their fundraising needs. Through this program, non-profit organizations received used guitars and turned them into beautiful and unique works of art that were then sold at auction. This is indicative of guitar companies across the board like Godin and Gretsch that have used their industry standing in order to give back to the community around them. Gibson and Fender also have community initiatives that work to put instruments in the hands of urban and underprivileged youth. Many studies have shown that a child who learns a musical instrument at a young age will do better in school, learn math and humanities more easily, and live a more productive life.

After 125 years, the Grestch family is still producing instruments, remaining active in the music community, and through their efforts with Fender, remain relevant. Grestch guitars have been seen in the hands of such artists as, Chris Cornell, Jim Heath (The Reverend Horton Heat), John Frusciante (Red Hot Chili Peppers), and Dave Grohl (Foo Fighters). All of this is thanks to a signature look and hardware - a body style that draws in a guitar player well before the headstock is ever seen, signifying the guitar as a Gretsch. "That Gretsch Sound" is what has kept the Gretsch running within a pack of companies that have ever-shrinking owners and smaller circles of production.

Opposite page: Elvis Costello playing Gretsch White Falcon guitar

Guild

GAD-F40

The Guild GAD-F40 guitar has an original grand orchestra all solid wood body based on the 1955 F-40 Valencia body shape, with a 16" lower bout, Sitka spruce top, flame maple back and sides, ebony fingerboard and bridge, bone nut and saddle, ebony bridge pins, wood binding and 1-11/16" nut. The F40 is representative of the Guild line of acoustics as a whole, though these have grown increasingly rare with Guild stopping production of its most recent models.

What is noticeable instantly about the GAD-F40 is the immense volume, which can be produced from the Grand Concert body style, and the playability of the instrument versus the more restrictive stance that is used when playing the larger dreadnought body types.

History of Acoustic Excellence

Guild's signature excellence in acoustic flat-top guitar design has made its name synonymous with fine quality and craftsmanship.

From three models introduced in 1954 The F-30 Aragon, F-40 Valencia and F-50 Navarre, Guild founded a business with real staying power in the music industry. The now famous D-40 Bluegrass Jubilee and D-50 Bluegrass Special dreadnoughts were introduced in 1963 (at the insistence of Guild veteran Mark Dronge, Al's son), and Guild's flagship dreadnought, the D-55, first appeared in 1968. These, and many other Guild six and twelve string acoustic flat-tops enjoyed widespread use and acclaim (from artists and amateurs alike) well into the modern era because of their technological leaps in production methods.

In the tumult that was the 1960s, Richie Havens was probably the foremost proponent of Guild acoustic guitars - a masterful interpreter and a soulful, electrifying performer who opened rock's legendary 1969 Woodstock festival by single-handedly mesmerizing the audience of 400,000 with his powerful voice and a Guild D-40, on which he displayed his trademark breathtaking rhythmic force. His performance of "Freedom" was a watershed moment for Havens, and one that Guild was able to take full advantage of. He continues to pack clubs and entertain audiences to this day with Guild guitars.

Musicians unknowingly make the perfect ambassadors for guitar companies by simply playing on the instruments that suit them best. Sometimes, this can be luck of the draw, or for some companies (like the previously mentioned Gretsch) it is a marketing strategy.

After nearly 30 years in Rhode Island (originally based in New Jersey), Guild was forced move the company west. Operations were moved to Corona, California shortly after Guild was acquired by the Fender Musical Instruments Corporation in 1995. This was the beginning of a new chapter in Guild history, and a move that was indicative of Fender's new business strategy of acquiring quality guitar companies to direct the right way. Guild has not suffered from the move at all.

Guild acoustic guitars have become the vehicle for many artists' musical expression: Hank Williams III, Willy Porter, and Cassandra Wilson are just some the artists that have ridden a Guild to prominence and musical acclaim. Recording studios and concert halls everywhere continue to reverberate with the full, instantly recognizable tone of Guild guitars. Whereas other companies have left the acoustic guitar behind, Guild retains a workshop that has nurtured the instrument and cradled it into the 21st century.

Opposite page: Johnny Cash performing on stage with his D605BE Guild guitar

GAD-5N

The Guild GAD-5N nylon string acoustic electric guitar has a cutaway, 14-fret neck joint, ebony fingerboard, 1 3/4" nut width, Seymour Duncan Timber-line pickup system, cedar top, solid African padauk back and sides, bone nut, bone compensated saddle, one-piece mahogany neck, all wood binding and purfling, rosewood bridge, ebony fingerboard, and 650 mm scale length.

The nylon string shows the versatility of Guild's luthiers as well as their dedication to the traditional aspect acoustic guitar design.

Its look is Spanish-inspired as it is modern in its construction. The wood choice represents a nod to the past with a guild tinge; cedar and spruce are traditional woods for guitar construction. However the inclusion of African padauk (a tree having edible leaves and containing a large amount of Vitamin C), is a possible homage to African tribal circles - one the wood's native uses.

From a Small Magazine Advertisement

In the April 1953 issue of Musical Merchandise Magazine, an advertisement was placed to mark the birth of a new guitar company, "A new corporation, known as Guild Guitars Inc., with headquarters at 220 Fourth Ave., New York, N.Y., has been formed to manufacture high-quality guitars, including Spanish and Hawaiian electric — solid wood body electrics, amplifiers, cases and strings." The ad was indeed small though it served its purpose: to show that once again, a small homespun company had the desire to make it big, and at that time in American history, almost anything was possible.

Created in October 1952, the infant Guild Guitars company set up a 1,500 square foot manufacturing facility on the second floor of a factory at 536 Pearl St., not far from where Guild founder Al Dronge's Park Row music store was set up in the 1930s and '40s. Avram "Alfred" Dronge, known simply as "Al" to many of his friends, was born in Warsaw, Poland, in 1911. His family left Warsaw for Paris in 1914, and left Paris for New York City in 1916. Dronge spent a significant amount of his youth in Manhattan's Park Row music stores, becoming an accomplished banjo player and guitarist to make effective use of his time.

Dronge gave guitar lessons and played professionally in New York clubs and on cruise ships, and opened his own successful Park Row music store in the mid-1930s. An astute, hardworking and well liked businessman, he sold the store in 1948 and amassed a small fortune (which was enough to retire on in the late '40s and early '50s) importing and distributing accordions.

How Guild became a company is a simple story. In 1952, Dronge's friend George Mann suggested that the two men start a new guitar company. Another friend of Dronge's, Gene Detgen, suggested the name "Guild", and the company was born. Guild was in business, with Mann and Dronge as president and vice president, in another corporate decision born from the simplest of sensibilities. Their first price list and catalog referenced Guild as building acoustic guitars crafted with the same skill and attention to craft as the world's most precious violins. By the end of the 1950s, arch-top acoustics had been added to Guid's line of flat-top and electrics, with the company being steered solely by Dronge.

GAD-C3

The Guild GAD-C3 Flamenco Negra guitar has a solid American Sitka top, solid Indian rosewood back and sides, bone nut, bone compensated saddle, one-piece mahogany neck, all wood binding and multicolored purfling, ebony fingerboard, rosewood bridge, 52 mm nut width, and 650 mm scale length. This acoustic guitar bears a resemblance to the Guild 5N in size and body design though the C3 lacks a pickup system or pre-amp. What changes for an acoustic guitar when it lacks those electronic components is the choice of its construction materials, the wood. Sitka spruce (used by Gibson and Fender) and Indian rosewood are used for the C3s body build and show that the company is willing to take no chances with regard to the quality of their acoustic guitars.

What is continually striking about acoustic guitar production, that acoustic/electric versus pure acoustic battle, is the price difference. There really isn't one. From company to company prices of instruments vary with quality and construction though within each given organization, the price difference is almost negligible in similar models where one is electrified and the other is not. The Guild C3 and 5N retail for the same price at many music stores. So, all things being equal, the modern era is becoming the perfect time for the guitar player to choose their purchase solely based on musical preference as opposed to the depth of their pockets.

Guild in the Future

Today's Guild owes a lot to Fender's distribution resources and marketing wing. They have been able to retain viability and heritage of old-world craftsmanship, modern design innovation and solid value due to a parent company who understands the realm of guitar sales - building them and putting them in the hands of young guitar players to build name loyalty.

In a continuing quest for operational expansion, Guild has moved again in recent years; from Corona, California to Tacoma, Washington in 2005, and most recently from Tacoma to a newly acquired facility in New Hartford, Connecticut in 2008. These are more traditional timber locations and carry the cost of production more easily.

The Acoustic Guitar in the Home

Accessibility and, perhaps more importantly, portability has lent much to the guitar's rise as the instrument of choice for the everyday. Whereas a piano is very much a static instrument in the home (aside from electronic keyboards - which are still cumbersome), the guitar, particularly the acoustic guitar, moves with the musician and is not chained to wall outlet or the length of a cord. Its voice carries its sound throughout rooms and over crowds. The musician is able to roam where they choose, play what they like and be wherever the energy conducive to creativity is best.

Opposite page: Justin Hayward, performing live onstage on Marty Wilde's 50th Anniversary Tour on May 27 at the Palladium

Hohner

DR 550

The new 500 Series acoustic guitars from Hohner were designed with one craft in mind - making music. From the classic binding and appointments, to the Grover tuning machines, to the optional Fishman Classic 4-T Blend preamp system, the 500 Series are perfect for stage and studio and offer rich, warm tones. The electronic improvements are a move in the right direction from a company that is not traditionally a strong guitar producer. That is not to say that Hohner has been a company of lax production methods and craft (quite to the contrary), but their strengths have often rested with other musical endeavors.

A Bumpy Road

Founded in 1857, Hohner is both the oldest and largest harmonica producer in the world. Thirty years after their founding, Hohner was producing more than 85,000 harmonicas a year. The years have seen the once exclusively produced instrument give rise to other products, including recorders, accordions, percussion instruments, and, more recently, guitars. The rise of rock and roll would force Hohner to add guitars to their more traditional harmonica and accordion production, in the face of shrinking sales and revenue bloodletting. At first, however, they were not the quickest to adapt to the popularity and universal appeal of the guitar.

By the 1960s it was clear that Hohner as a company had missed the boat on the acoustic/electric guitar movement worldwide. Ernest Hohner, the CEO of the family-owned company at the time, did not provide Hohner with enough lateral movement and bounce to create eye catching and musically relevant instruments. He believed rock and roll to be a fad, the guitar being the flag bearer for a movement that would be a flash in the pan. Thankfully for Hohner, his retirement in 1965 marked the path for a new direction. The DR 550 is proof that the path was, at the very least, walked down.

The ensuing decades would see Hohner finally pursue guitar production in greater earnest, as well moving as some of their harmonica production to the United States. Forming Hohner/HSS with Sonor and Sabian, the United States division of Hohner began to distribute guitars and cymbals. Hohner also began to produce guitars under its own brand, as well. Revenues for Hohner still continued to shrink despite these changes, reaching a tipping point by 1986. Hohner was forced to make significant layoffs, and Kunz-Holding GmbH & Co. obtained a controlling interest in Hohner around the same time.

The Guitar is a Lesson

"Give the customer what they want" has been the overriding message of American businesses in general, since the Industrial Revolution. This is no less true of guitar companies that have recruited master luthiers in a drive to create not only the highest quality instruments, but ultimately instruments that are marketable, and one that the guitar player will buy. After all; no guitars, no money, and no money, no guitars. Companies like Gibson, Fender, Avalrez have shown off their mobility in their chameleon-like ability to innovate and resist stagnancy within their own markets which has allowed for greater improvement within the acoustic realm of guitars as well as electrics, amps, and so on.

HW 90

Dreadnought Acoustic Solid Spruce Top Scalloped X-braced top Pearloid O Series position markers & bridge inlay Tortoiseshell pickguard 2-way adjustable tension rod 20 frets Gold die-cast tuning machines with amber pearloid buttons. Hohner uses exclusively seasoned and hand-picked wood to manufacture guitars. The activemusician.com writes of the HW 90,"rare and exotic woods are used to create a resonant, bright sounding instrument that is also rich in depth of tone and increased sustain. Hohner's patented scalloped X-braced top allows for the guitar to resonate more than the average guitar, and as a bonus, this method of construction makes the instrument stronger and increases its life span."

Sounds like a company line, down to the letter. While it is true that the scalloping of the X-brace design allows for greater resonance and vibration within an acoustic guitar, it is hardly the exclusive provenance of Hohner, with the company being such a latecomer to guitar design and production. Nearly every company covered, every guitar examined, has a version of their company's "patented" or "exclusive" X-bracing design. As well, the woods used in the building of Hohner's instruments are very rare, though no less uncommon than the woods used in other acoustic guitars through the 1800s to the present. A large percentage of the instruments examined here have a body made from Sitka spruce, or mahogany, have ebony for their fingerboards or rosewood. All this should tell the guitar player is that Hohner is at last on par with its competitors, though far from leading them.

How Hohner Has Survived All This Weather

In 1997, Taiwan based K.H.S. Musical Instruments Co. Ltd. purchased the majority of Kunz-Holding's share in Hohner. This change would mark the recovery of Hohner, posting a profit in 2001. Changes to production saw lower priced models having production moved overseas from Germany, while higher quality instruments, including new models of guitar, like the Hohner Black Prince (an electric baring a suspiciously Telecaster-like body style) and Artist Elite, continued production in Europe.

Hohner's guitars on the American market are regularly half of the cost of American made acoustic instruments. This is the hallmark of instruments produced abroad in larger Eastern countries.

The changes to production are most likely a result of a shift in production centers from a European model of construction to a Taiwanese one, which features lower labor cost and sizeable work force. Though as we have seen an increase in productivity leads to increased profits (illustrated by Hohner's profit posting in '01), it may also lead to lower overall instrument quality – something others have found in acoustic guitars that have been built abroad rather than by the hands of skilled luthier who has devoted a lifetime of learning to their craft. The guitar is as much a statement of artistic expression as a painting or sculpture. It takes creativity to realize the image, and shape it into a living entity that produces more than the sum of its parts.

HC09TE

Probably the most affordable nylon string, Spanish-inspired acoustic guitar on the market today, the Hohner HC09TE, part of Hohner's Classical guitar line, is designed for a variety of player levels and budgets, but all in the name of offering the same high level of craftsmanship and loyalty of sound as higher end models. The HC09TE features traditional appointments and classical styling, coupled with a Shadow P-3 Preamp system - allowing the player to connect with their audience in any live or studio setting.

The instrument is decked out with the following specifications: the body style is a thin-line, though it features a classical shape, and the slender body profile allows for increased playability for the smaller musician. Its top is spruce with the back and sides being composed of mahogany, which is offset by the black ivoroid which serves as the body binding. The neck is mahogany, and the fingerboard, solid rosewood. Rosewood tuners round out the motif, creating a classic look with real economy in mind. Notice the absence of mother of pearl, which is used in higher end, domestically produced models, in favor of the more fiscally responsible "ivoroid." Hohner has designed an acoustic guitar for economically harder times.

Alone or in a crowd, wherever you go, whatever you do, take a Hohner, the harmonica of the stars. Easy to learn with the *free* 5-minute tutor leaflet. From all music dealers.

It's fun to own a

HOHNER

HARMONICAS & ACCORDIONS
The world's best

Hohner in the Right Direction

As a guitar producer, Hohner lacks the stateside credibility of the more established guitar manufacturers such as Guild, Fender, and Gibson. This is in part due to their late arrival in the acoustic guitar/electric guitar scene and to the unreliable production methods of offshore factories. What makes these homegrown, domestically based (Godin included) companies so successful with guitar players is their consistent drive for maintenance of quality. Hohner has found a way to stay in the game with technological advances, the use of Fishman electronics and Shadow P-3 systems, but as far as innovation is concerned, they are they are falling behind the pack.

The acoustic guitar has many international credentials, and has been built and developed in many countries, but for Hohner, their lack of vision (with regard to rock and roll in particular) has lead to a game of catch up with their competitors. It will be interesting to see over time, in which direction the European based company takes off, and whether or not it will be able to listen to the will of the people as deftly as other guitar workshops have.

Hohner has built many a fine harmonica, and there are many skilled and quite famous harmonica players around who play them. Who can forget the image of Bob Dylan holding an acoustic guitar with a harmonica strapped to his shoulders, or John Popper whaling away with Blues Traveler? These are passing images of accompaniment however, as it is clear that at least in the years since World War II, through the sixties, and all the way into our present, the guitar is king here.

Ibanez

Above: Pat Metheny performing
stage, playing an Ibanez guitar

Ambiance A100EBK

The Ibanez A100EBK Ambiance acoustic electric guitar is a good live performance guitar, built with an eye tuned towards garnering attention. The acoustic is kitted out with a comfortable neck, Fishman Aero preamp with onboard tuner and balanced 1/4" and XLR outputs, a large, resonant arched back, and overall, produces warm resonant tones.

This latest Ibanez Ambiance series of acoustic electric guitars is designed for the guitarist with a mind for the stage, or just any serious acoustic guitar player who needs an acoustic electric guitar with superior electronics. An onboard chromatic tuner and balanced 1/4" and XLR connectors makes the Ambiance line very versatile for live performances, where speed and convenience are the easiest routes to a stress-free live show. The onboard tuner on the Ibanez A100EBK acoustic guitar is very easy to use, and works as advertised, which is not always the case for some tuners. The tuner indicates the string being tuned and the "in tune" light turns green when the correct pitch is reached.

With a continued look into the A100EBK electric acoustic guitar, it also features an Ivorex II nut, which is stronger and more durable than bone and is more commonly used on handmade acoustic guitars. Ivorex II allows for brighter highs and more pronounced lows with less mid-range, making Ivorex II-fitted guitars perfect for amplification. The Ibanez A100E acoustic guitar is beautifully finished with a high gloss that makes it a standout in any room. This Ibanez line illustrates the true march of technology as it works its way into the very materials that are used to build the acoustic guitar. We still see spruce and mahogany being used for the body construction but it coincides with the slow removal of less than renewable resources: bone, sinew etc.

Who is Ibanez Guitars?

It began in 1908 with Hoshino, a company selling sheet music out of a storefront in Nagoya, Japan. The Ibanez brand name dates back to 1929 when Hoshino Gakki (founder of the company that bore his name) began importing Salvador Ibanez guitars from Spain. When the Salvador Ibáñez workshop was destroyed during the Spanish Civil War in the early part of the 1900s, Ibanez guitars were obviously no longer available, so Hoshino Gakki bought the "Ibanez Salvador" brand name and rights, and started making Spanish-styled acoustic guitars in 1935, at first using the "Ibanez Salvador" brand name, later shortening it to "Ibanez".

In the company's infancy, Hoshino copied existing European guitar body designs. This continued into the fifties and sixties when Hoshino (now distributing under the Ibanez name) began exporting guitars to the United States which featured interesting body designs in an attempt to find a niche in the guitar world. Some actually made it to department stores and were sold to the public. When this attempt to catch the American eye failed, Ibanez turned to copying existing body designs. Ibanez labeled copies of Gibson, Fender, and Rickenbacker guitar designs soon began to appear in stores.

Ibanez

Montage MSC650VV

The Ibanez MSC650VV Montage Series Cutaway Acoustic-Electric is a revolutionary guitar that has two acoustic sounds, 2 electric sounds, mix capability, onboard reverb, chorus, distortion, phase canceling, dual notch filter and tuner. These groundbreaking, innovative electronics are possible with the combination of the B-Band UST Acoustic Pickup, Ibanez AP9 Electric pickup, and the Ibanez HBP Multi-function Preamp with Onboard Tuner. Controls are conveniently mounted on the face of the upper bout. It operates on 4 AA batteries and has a 4" balanced output.

The MSC650VV guitar also features a quilted maple body with a vintage violin gloss finish. Montage series guitars have a sleek, comfortable cutaway semi-jumbo body style and the exclusive Ibanez adjustable mahogany F.A.S.T. (Fast Action Set-Up Technology) lets the player quickly set up according to their personal playing style. Other appointments include a rosewood fingerboard and bridge, Advantage bridge pins, and gold die-cast tuners. The guitar, as an acoustic, is visually stunning and shows a similarity to the art pieces produced by Canadian based Godin, though Ibanez shows a greater flare for the electronic aspects of guitar sound production.

Ibanez Through The '70s And Beyond

The period immediately following the 1960s is sometimes referred to as the "Ibanez lawsuit period." Needless to say, American guitar companies were not pleased with Ibanez producing guitars which copied their seminal body styles and signature acoustic/electric models. The successful lawsuits that followed deterred Ibanez from this practice, as well as other lesser-known guitar companies that were producing body styles synonymous (and copyrighted) with more famous guitar companies.

Hoshino Gakki also had semi acoustic, nylon and steel stringed acoustic guitars manufactured under the Ibanez name. Tama acoustic guitars were made from 1974-1979 at the Tama Drum factory. In 1979 the Tama acoustic guitars were renamed as the Artwood Series and were also made at the Tama Drum factory. Most Ibanez guitars were made for Hoshino Gakki by the FujiGen guitar factory in Japan up until the mid to late 1980s and from then on Ibanez guitars have also been manufactured in other Asian countries such as Korea, China and Indonesia. During the early 1980s the FujiGen guitar factory also produced most of the Roland guitar synthesizers including the Stratocaster-style Roland G-505, the twin humbucker Roland G-202 and the Ibanez X-ING IMG-2010.

By the mid-80s, with the interest in instrumental rock guitars on the rise, Ibanez collaborated with players such as Steve Vai, Joe Satriani and Paul Gilbert, and brought out the JEM, JS, RG and S models. Today, present day versions such as these models still are considered the standard in hard rock and instrumental rock guitars. Ibanez has rightly made a name for itself in that niche of guitar production - crafting instruments with the "professional player", or virtuoso, in mind. This is no less true of the Montage, though even more so with the Ambiance series of acoustic guitars.

EW40CBENT

The Ibanez EW40CBENT acoustic electric guitar has a Cocobolo body, with a rich, deep glow to the finish. This guitar does certainly look the part, and thanks to Ibanez's dedication to electronic integration, it sounds it as well. Tonality and playability are the two most important factors that go into the design and production of an acoustic guitar, the Ibanez Exotic Wood Series (EW) has both. They stand out visually and sonically, and have been built with the intention of enhancing the performing musician's tonal artillery.

The appearance and sound of the Ibanez EW series acoustic electric guitars were designed for the guitarist who is looking for a completely new and different voice - a true attention getter. You won't find anything else quite like the new EW series guitars from Ibanez- a perfect balance of classic design and exotic beauty. The Ibanez EW40CBENT features the EW body shape with cutaway, and is complimented by a beautiful natural high gloss finish.

What is Cocobolo?

Cocobolo is a tropical hardwood from Central America. Only the heartwood is used in manufacturing. This is typically orange or reddish-brown in color, often with a figuring of darker irregular traces weaving through the wood. By contrast, the sapwood (not used) is a creamy yellow, with a sharp boundary with the heartwood. The heartwood is known to change color after being cut, lending to its appeal. Its use with the EW40 produces a guitar with an earthy feel yet deeply resonant tone.

Cocobolo is oily in look and feel, and stands up well to repeated handling and exposure to water: a common use is in gun grips and knife handles. It is very hard, fine textured and dense, but is easily machined, although due to the abundance of natural oils, the wood tends to clog abrasives and fine-toothed saw blades. Like other very hard, very dense tropical woods, due to its density and hardness, even a large block of the cut wood will produce a clear musical tone if struck. Cocobolo can be polished to a lustrous, glassy finish. The high natural oil content of the wood makes it difficult to achieve a strong glue joint, and can inhibit the curing process of some varnishes. It would seem even nature itself resists collection as it is quite common to have allergic reactions to the dust created from the tree's wood and oils produced from working it.

Forward-thinking Wood Experimentation

Ibanez's EW40 is a step in the right direction and is a far cry from the copying of existing body styles that occurred decades earlier. Here, the company has begun to do what other guitar creators and luthiers have also been doing recently - learning and experimenting with non-traditional tone woods, and getting away from the tried and dwindling supplies of spruce and mahogany (though it is still used for the neck). Ibanez has also laced their own electronics through the design, inserting an Ibanez designed SRTn preamp with an onboard tuner and notch filter into the EW40. Larger production scale favors Ibanez here as this visually appealing instrument is priced very competitively.

Ibanez

EW20'sGENT

The Ibanez EW20'sGENT acoustic electric guitar has a Spalted Mango wood body, and has a rich, deep glow to the finish. The EW series of Ibanez guitars are designed to look and sound unique, and the company has done a fair job at making both happen when it is in the hands of a skilled acoustic guitar player.

This particular Ibanez model appears as though it was pulled from the tree mere hours before. The rivets and cracks created from the acoustics' wood choice allows for the natural feel of the mango wood to shine as though in its natural elements. This is all done with cost in mind, with Ibanez employing a good deal of their signature/in-house electronics in order to keep the cost to the consumer at a reasonable level.

The Ibanez EW20'sGENT features the EW body shape with cutaway, and is complimented by a natural, high gloss finish, which plays counterpoint to the rustic look of the mango wood. It is rare to see such an affordable, attractive and musically viable instrument all in one. The EW series has been a move in the right direction for the guitar maker that was once litigated into an all-but halt of production.

Mango Wood as a Tonal Wood

The tree is known by its fruit, and this is no less true of mango wood. Its main areas of growth are Southeast Asia including Thailand. The wood accepts kiln drying fairly readily and this makes it easily worked and processed. As of 2007 mango wood had been gaining in use as a wood for manufacturing for several reasons: one being the mill-stoning of teak stocks throughout the Asian market, and two, the Thai government beginning to push for more exported goods produced in Thailand. While mango wood is softer than teak, it is very easily worked and painted, making it an ideal replacement wood.

Mango wood has traditionally been used for craft items such as candle holders and picture frames. Musically it is most often found as the framework for drums built in the Java region. The percussive quality of the wood lends itself to the acoustic guitar, which requires the body work to vibrate and sustain that vibration in order to produce adequate sound for even an electrified instrument to be worthwhile. Technology can do only so much.

The Very Latest from Ibanez

Steve Vai, guitar master and longtime signature artist for Ibanez has agreed to appear for the National Guitar Workshop at their Rock Summit in New York in 2009. As a Grammy award-winning guitar virtuoso, Steve Vai's sheer breathtaking skill on the guitar is acclaimed in the rock world and beyond. Starting with his groundbreaking "Passion and Warfare" album in 1990, and throughout the years since, Vai has consistently used music as a microscope peering into the human spirit, with equal attention paid to both the darkest obsessions and the most exalted impulses contained there. While Vai clearly had what was needed to make indelible impressions during his stays with Frank Zappa, David Lee Roth and Whitesnake, it's as a solo artist that he's made his most precious contributions.

EWC30PDERLG

The more compact member of the Ibanez Exotic Wood family, the EWC acoustic-electric features a body that is smaller in size and shallower than the original EW's, for increased playing comfort and acoustic projection. With a top of padauk, a mahogany neck and body, B-Band pickup and SRTn preamp with onboard tuner, the EWC30PDERLG guitar from the EW acoustic guitar family will inspire you with its great looks, sound and playability. The sharp cutaway is an Ibanez fueled example of their sound aesthetics, and provides easy access to the highest frets. Proprietary electronics give the guitar player control over their tone, and the 1/4" and XLR output give this model the versatility to plug into any amplification and still 'sound the part'.

What is so intriguing about this Ibanez line is its accessibility. Ibanez began as a company of copiers and has emerged as a workshop that produces instruments for the masters - the Steve Vais and Joe Satrianis of the world. However, these instruments of the EWC series show the luthier's ability to craft a unique instrument, while at the same time keeping the player's wallet in mind. Acoustic guitar players won't find anything else quite like the Ibanez EW guitars even among guitars that are much more expensive.

Where the Modern Acoustic Guitar Player Sits

There are many choices for the acoustic guitar player in the 21st century. Nearly every musical tradition, path or even a vague desire may be catered to and carried out well. Ibanez is representative of the wide swath that the acoustic guitar has been able to cut into the global musical consciousness; a company that began in Japan, importing Spanish guitars, that now produces instruments that the greatest modern guitar players have chosen as their own. What other product in the world can boast such a multi-cultural upbringing and appeal?

What is most important about all these companies is that they are all integral to the breadth of variety of acoustic guitars available. Each holds a facet of the greater puzzle that makes up the acoustic guitar and its marketing. Each must continue to exist in order for the full breadth of the musical pantheon to be made available. Ibanez is the perfect example of a guitar company without a niche that was essentially forced into innovation by the likes of Fender and Gibson. The existing companies have sent a message to all those that would seek to cause stagnation in the guitar's style and performance through imitation or outright forgery - those that will not push forward will be left behind.

Opposite page: Ibanez EWC 30 PD ERLG Acoustic guitar

Luna

Henna Paradise Spruce

"The pattern I chose for Luna's Paradise guitar is based on the art of Medieval Spain," says Henna Artist Alex Morgan on her artwork for the Henna Paradise, "The culturally rich and diverse period is the only one in which Henna was grown and used as a cosmetic in Europe. The era also was historically important in development and growing popularity of the guitar." Ornamenting the skin with henna is among the world's oldest known art forms. A paste is made from the henna plant (Lawsonia Inermis) and applied to the skin in a wide array of intricate designs. Luna Guitars is a workshop which is pushing the envelope from the acoustic guitar as an art form, to being a canvas for another. Their line of work is as visually stunning as it is thought provoking for the future of the instrument.

At the cutting edge of guitar production and design, Luna has employed laser etching technology to faithfully recreate the intricate design that renowned henna artist Alex Morgan envisioned specifically for the guitar company in these breathtaking instruments. The Henna Paradise Spruce's folk styling provides a perfect background that evokes the sensuous lines and curves that make henna body art such a beguiling form of expression. Rich woods and complex tones offer players a guitar that is as unforgettable in its craft as it is in its artistry. The Henna Paradise is built from quilted mahogany, solid spruce for its top, and rosewood adorns the fingerboard.

The History of Luna Guitars

Yvonne de Villiers was a stained glass artist when she envisioned the guitar company that would become Luna. This inspiration was generated from watching her mother, Hilda, play bass in several bands as she was growing up. Yvonne noticed her mother continually struggle with traditionally heavy electric basses as they weighed down her petite frame. Yvonne reached much the same conclusion that founded Daisy Rock Guitars: women should have guitars designed for their needs. Luna Guitars was founded in 2005, on the principles of creating visually captivating guitars that stimulate the minds and creative spirits of women as well as catering to their unique body design needs and skill sets.

"The moon has a cool, guiding light," she explains in an interview with dolphinmusic.co.uk, "I envisioned Luna embodying that same healing and enchanting essence. Not a hot look-at-me attitude, but a reflective look-at-yourself... you're beautiful quality. With that in mind, I feel that Luna Guitars and the individuals who play them will express each other perfectly." The guitar company is currently headquartered in Tampa, Florida, where it produces six and twelve string guitars. Recently, Luna created an acoustic guitar to the specifications of the current American Idol winner, David Cook.

Luna's mission statement is a simple one, "Our focus is on our customers, and we pledge our efforts to serving them responsively," writes Luna Guitars, "We actively encourage their interaction to refine and expand the design of our instrument lines and to influence the development of accessories and services to enhance their guitar playing experiences. We are committed to helping our customers achieve their musical goals and, we embrace the opportunity to contribute to their emotional and spiritual journeys, as well."

Opposite page: a closer look at the Luna Henna Paradise Spruce guitar

Luna

Luna Phoenix

The Phoenix features a solid Sitka spruce top with exquisite ebony inlay on soundboard and rosette to form the mythological bird and crescent moon design. An ebony bridge, bone saddle, ebony binding, mahogany back and sides and solid mahogany back complete the immaculately crafted body. Luna's premium mother-of-pearl logo shines brightly from an ebony headstock. Gotoh 18:1 chrome tuners with ebony buttons offer preciseness, ease and elegance.

Luna's premium mother-of-pearl signature moon phase fret markers trace the length of the ebony fret board over a one piece mahogany neck crowned by a bone nut. From ancient Egyptian tales to Native American lore to the mysterious legends of Arabia, the phoenix has soared through many cultures and times. Depicted as a magnificent bird that rises from the ashes of its own pyre to live again, the phoenix's alluring song was said to mesmerize even the great god Apollo. A symbol of rebirth, the phoenix represents beauty, power, vision and inspiration.

Complimenting the design effort is the inclusion of a state-of-the-art B-Band preamp tuner that maintains the intimate and natural acoustic tonal quality of these fine instruments. The preamp includes a 3 band EQ, phase select, low cut filter with frequency select, as well as Hi and Lo Z outputs.

Luna Making a Difference

As a guitar manufacturer, Luna appears to be walking the walk. They employ a specially designed neck profile for ease in playability and access to the fret board. Lighter woods are used in their guitar making as well, so that longer sets are handled without breaking a sweat. Luna was also the first guitar company to take laser etching from around the soundhole rosette to using the entire front, back, and headstock as a canvas. Their guitar makers have taken traditional inlay around the soundhole and have experimented with freeform inlay at sound hole, employing the actual body of the guitar. They have truly turned the entire guitar into a painting - a work of art from head stock to strap button.

Just as we saw Ibanez innovating electronically, here we see Luna doing the same work on the artistic side of guitar production. It is interesting that up until this company surfaced very recently, the acoustic guitar was largely utilitarian in construction. Yes, tonal woods have very unique looks and were often employed in the service of beautifying the instrument, and there are companies that have been working long and hard to improve the aesthetic appeal of the acoustic guitar. However, Luna has done it from the outside in (rather than focus on innovative construction), though they have certainly done a small amount of that as well in their work on soundhole construction. Luna is also a part of a culture shift just like Daisy Rock Guitars, in that that they are bridging gender gaps in luthiery, marketing, and playability of the acoustic guitar. The "manly" dreadnought and jumbo styles are being rethought, reinvented, and moved into a mode that reflects societal shifts.

Opposite Page: a closer look at the
Luna 'artist' Phoenix guitar

Luna

The Trinity

Another guitar by Luna has American Idol ties. The Trinity acoustic made its television debut when it played live by Idol finalist Jason Castro. The Trinity balances Luna's best creative and technical efforts. Crafted at the historic Terada, Japan factory that has manufactured guitars for Alvarez, Gibson, Gretsch, and Martin, the Luna Trinity combines uncompromising structural integrity and superb playability with tone and projection worthy of any professional artist or discriminating player. This is a company with a world scope, and one that has built an impressive portfolio of work in very little time.

The Trinity features a solid Sitka spruce top with an extraordinary knot work design at the sound hole crafted of mother-of-pearl with ebony borders. An ebony bridge, classic herringbone binding, rosewood sides and solid rosewood back put the finishing touches on this elegant instrument. Luna's crescent moon mother-of-pearl logo shines brightly from an ebony headstock with Gotoh 18:1 tuners. The company's signature mother-of-pearl moon phase fret markers make their way down an ebony fret board with stainless steel frets. Luna's attention to detail is further evidenced by a bone nut and saddle. Luna has managed to create instruments using industry-standard materials and still create work in the image of their founder's one-time art. Like stained glass, each Luna guitar comprises a small piece of the company's larger goal of changing the musical landscape to one that is more inclusive.

Complementing the Trinity's design is the inclusion of a state-of-the-art B-Band Preamp tuner that maintains the intimate and natural acoustic tonal quality of the fine instrument. The Preamp includes a 3-band equalizer, phase select, low cut filter with frequency select, as well as Hi and Lo Z outputs. Luna's artist series is comprised of the Trinity, the Phoenix, and the Henna Acatha designs that have been featured thus far.

Opposite page: a closer look at the Luna The Trinity guitar

Television is the Guitar's Best Friend

The guitar has benefited immeasurably from the advent of television and film. Digital Technology has taken the accessibility of images of guitars, and those artists that play them to the widest audience imaginable, and provided those burgeoning players with the guitars that their heroes have played at gigs and on widely broadcasted videos. Rickenbacker and Hofner could not keep their instruments in department stores after the Beatles premiered on the Ed Sullivan Show in America, just as the images of Jimi Hendrix holding a Fender Stratocaster have become inseparable from the guitar manufacturer.

Digital media creates a means by which musicians may share music in real time, collaborate and learn together. This causes the musical community to mutate, become more integrated, with styles blurring and edges fusing into one another. We have seen this throughout the decades in the birth and meld of musical movements - from the advent of punk rock in the '70s, to the rise of rap and hip hop, and later the merge of the two. As music and artists that create it begin to collaborate, it causes a need for their musical instruments to change as well. The acoustic guitar has continually shown the ability to accept new technology, adapt, remain relevant and retain the intimacy involved in creating with it.

Luna

Oracle Zen

An oracle was a priest or priestess acting as a medium through which advice or prophecy was sought from the gods in realms of Ancient Greece. An oracle may also be said to be a person or thing regarded as an infallible authority or guide. Following Luna's innovative tradition, The Oracle Series foresees the future of guitar architecture and takes solid top guitar ornamentation into uncharted territory - mapping out the art of the guitar as the entire instrument, not just the finish.

Zen is the practice of mindfulness. Through meditation one is able to find their personal center, allowing thoughts to flow free-form through meditation without grasp or retention. In effect, Zen is nothing, as much as the mind is here and yet not visible. Luna's Zen inspires the mind through its unique features and pioneering design. Essentially, the player approaches the instrument differently, because this acoustic guitar looks like no other.

The maple fingerboard is inlaid with rosewood calligraphy that reads Wisdom, Beauty, Truth, Courage, Grace, Peace and Love. Calligraphy ensconced on the heel cap translates Light, which is intrinsic to Luna's mission. The sound hole is surrounded by a rosewood inlaid bagua against a solid Sitka spruce top.

The Stability of the Body Style

At this point in its history the acoustic guitar's body styles have been fairly well fleshed out, meaning that we have a stable number of consistent building dimensions that work for the guitar player as well as the luthier making them. This has several advantages. It allows for greater speed in production as the luthier and larger guitar manufacturer are not working on invention but innovation. Innovation is possible through the stability in the form the "now we've got one thing figured out, we can work on another" strategy. Luna Guitars is the manifestation of this stability.

We must be careful to the avoid terms like "stagnation" when it comes to areas of body design. There are other companies (Guild being one) that are working on slight tweaks to the traditional dreadnought, jumbo, and grand concert body styles, however none are seeking to completely change the way the guitar is constructed or seen. Experimental body design has always been the province of the electric guitar, where technology and hardware play an inseparable role in its creation. The acoustic guitar is a stable instrument in terms of body design (the greatest innovation since the 1900s being the X-brace system) which allows companies like Luna to create beautiful designs - amazing inlays that are considered true pieces of art because they're not worried if the guitar will be able to resonate properly. That work has already been done, and modern companies now reap the benefits.

Of course, if the guitar sounds awful, it will not matter what it looks like. Luna has been able to look at those that have come before for the template for success. Look at their construction methods: keep the art projects in-house, move the higher selling models to offshore factories to reduce costs, and use time honored woods like spruce and mahogany. The rest will take care of itself.

*Opposite page: a closer look
at the Luna Oracle Zen guitar*

Fauna Dragon

Curled across the face of the guitar in iridescent abalone, the eldritch creature projects the brooding sense of power that is its legacy. Serpent of myth, the dragon is a hoarder of gold and keeper of lost knowledge and magic. The rich abalone Dragon inlay winds its way across the guitar's raven finish, making this instrument the focus of the action from the moment it comes out of the case. If there were an acoustic guitar built for the showman that exists in every stage performer, the Fauna Dragon would be on the list.

Luna's specially designed neck profile ensures a comfortable playing experience that puts challenging notes and chords within easy reach. Luna's exclusive moon phase fret board markers, inlaid in abalone, trace the length of the rosewood fret board over mahogany neck. The guitar company's in-house Orion 4-band preamp provides the very latest in playing versatility. When a player's acoustic mood turns electric, the unit provides more than enough power for any setting, and the equalizer allows the player to shape the sound to their exact desire and specifications. The electronics include a built-in tuner to take the guesswork out of a flawlessly tuned guitar.

The Fauna Dragon Folk Acoustic-Electric Guitar has a downsized jumbo cutaway body that is comfortably contoured to fit any musician. The Fauna Dragon has a select spruce top for a full range of sound, and the sides and back have been crafted from mahogany. The Dragon features Luna's gently curved headstock with a signature crescent moon logo inlaid in sparkling abalone. Matte nickel die-cast tuners provide smooth and precise adjustment.

This instrument is extremely affordable, which only adds to its appeal. There are many guitars on the market that are built from fine woods, elite electronics, and crafted by the most skilled luthiers and manufacturers. These guitars are true prizes, and it is rare that the everyday musician has the capital to afford such a quality six string. The Luna Fauna Dragon combines a rare element of beauty, craft and affordability.

Guitars in the Series

The Dragon is part of the larger Fauna series of acoustic guitars produced by Luna. This also bears significance within the company and contributes to the inspiration of the line. Fauna was the Roman goddess of the Earth and the wild creatures that dwelt within it. There would seem to be no mythical creature that is its own master the way that the dragon has been perceived to be. Luna also takes elements from Eastern religion in the crafting of the Dragon. As the Phoenix appears in Greece it also appears in Far East, just as the Dragon does. The Phoenix embodies the spirit of Yin, the Dragon is the Yang. So it stands to reason that if one guitar be built, the other must also be brought into the light in order to maintain the balance of both. Luna is a guitar company working well in balance: with its players, luthiers, and the world at large.

*Opposite page: a closer look at the
Luna Fauna Dragon guitar*

Martin

The D-28

Some would call C.F Martin & Co the acoustic guitar company that started it all; the very crème of all crops that will ever be produced. For every guitar company that would claim to be an innovator, it is Martin from which they draw their blueprints. They are the originators of the Dreadnought body style, and the scalloped X-bracing system. In a line of popular guitars, Martin's most popular is the D-28, and it has been so since the model's inception in the early 1900s.

"In 1931 C.F. Martin introduced the D body shape guitars," writes Graham Lee for suite101.com, "the D-1 and the D-2. The D stands for Dreadnought, the largest British battleship. Extremely limited numbers of the D-1 and D-2 were made, so limited that these guitars must be the most collectable acoustics of all. When the guitar went into a proper production cycle it was slotted into the familiar Martin guitar numbering system - a letter of the alphabet to designate body size and shape followed by a number to indicate the style of finish and woods used. The D-18 was less ornate and had a mahogany back and sides paired with dark body bindings, while the D-28 used Brazilian rosewood for the back and sides and had herringbone trim and a zipper style back stripe. More expensive models - the D-35 and D-45 were produced but it was the D-28 that found its way into the hearts of guitarists from all spheres."

Many popular musicians have played D-28s to career record sales and face time. Several members of The Beatles, as well as Elvis Presley have all played the iconic instrument on some of their most famous tracks, thus cementing the legend of Martin's flagship instrument.

Martin in the New World

C.F Martin was born in 1796 in Germany. His predecessors had been cabinet makers and other wood craftsmen, though his father was also a luthier. At an early age Martin's father had him apprenticed to a very well known guitar maker in Vienna, where he trained and learned the craft. Upon completion, C.F returned to his hometown where he set up shop and began to build his own instruments. The guitar, at that time in history, was the child of the music industry, and thought of very little as a classical instrument of any value. As such, it was controlled (as per Europe's guild system at the time) by the cabinet maker's guild. A problem arose when the Violinist's Guild began to claim exclusive rights over the production of musical instruments. They tried three times to litigate away the cabinet maker's right to produce guitars, thrice failing. All the legal warbling soured C.F Martin's taste with the guild system in Europe, and he was soon on a ship headed for the North American coast.

By 1833 Martin had moved his fledgling business to the New World, settling at first in New York City, though by 1838 had the company moved to its present day home in Nazareth, Pennsylvania.

Above right: Pete Townshend
from The Who, posed, playing
his Martin
Opposite page: Elvis Presley
performs on stage with his
brand new Martin D-28
acoustic guitar

Martin

D-35 Johnny Cash

The Martin D-35 Johnny Cash Commemorative guitar's polished-black gloss lacquer finish allows its best features to show through quite easily. Five bands of alternating black and white purfling encircle the top, three bands encircle the back and five bands border the sides, in all cases protected by grained ivoroid binding. The grained ivoroid heel cap and endpiece are likewise framed by multiple black and white inlays. The Style 45 rosette features an inlay of specially chosen green abalone pearl. Traditional Style 35 "zigzag" back strips separate the three-piece back.

Both the fingerboard and headstock are bound with grained ivoroid (stronger than bone synthetic) and inset with mitered black/white fine line inlays. Martin's Old Style large decal logo gleams on the polished black Ebony head plate. True to Cash's D-35 Custom, the headstock also sports Grover Rotomatic enclosed chrome tuners. The African black Ebony fingerboard is inlaid with position markers similar to those on the D-42 Johnny Cash Signature Edition and small abalone stars bordered with mother of pearl at the 5th, 7th, 9th, 12th and 15th frets. Johnny Cash's signature in pearl appears between the 19th and 20th frets.

The D-35 Johnny Cash Commemorative bares a quality that is without question and a sound that instantly recognizable. Combining an Engelmann spruce top with 1/4" forward shifted scalloped braces gives this Dreadnought sugar-like tone and industry best responsiveness. Back and sides of East Indian rosewood add warmth and projection. The 1-11/16" neck is carved from genuine mahogany. A bone nut and compensated bone saddle (fitted in an ebony belly bridge), enhance its resounding power and clarity. Abalone-topped black Style 42 bridge pins and endpin add an elegant touch of color. A polished and beveled black serves as protection for the guitar's top.

For the "man in black" a black guitar case as well; specifically a Geib style case with special black hardware and a black interior. The D-35 Johnny Cash Commemorative guitar arrives stock with a special interior label in tribute to the "Man in Black," each personally signed by Cash's son, John Carter Cash and Martin Chairman C. F. Martin IV, numbered in sequence.

The Tribute Guitar for a Legend

The black dreadnought built for Cash in 1972 was another seminal release for Martin. Factory employees were forced to remain vigilant while crafting this guitar, keeping it hidden from C.F. Martin III who was the president of the company at the time. He believed the idea of a "black" Martin acoustic was too out of left field for the company to tackle. As Cash made an appearance on the hard-boiled detective "dramedy", Columbo, the clandestine black dreadnought was revealed.

The D-35 Johnny Cash is not Martin's first Cash signature model. The company offered a limited edition Cash D-35 Custom in 1989, and a D-42JC in '97. Cash himself played these and other Martins (more often than not, the D-35 models) throughout his career. One acoustic guitar in particular was his late sixties D-35S, which he had designed with ornate abalone inlay on the headstock and custom acorn and leaf designs along the guitar's fingerboard.

Above: Martin D-35 acoustic guitar
Opposite page: Johnny Cash on his black D-35

Martin

D-100 Deluxe

Easily the most expensive acoustic guitar on the market today or at any time, the D-100 Deluxe boasts a price tag containing (depending on retailer) six figures. For this glut of cash, the musician can buy a piece of history.

The D-100 was created following the release of Martin's 1,000,000th guitar and bears the first fifty sequential numbers following that guitar's run off the luthier's workshop line. This dreadnought owes much to the designer of that millionth model, Larry Robinson, whose intricate inlay work contributes in large part to the mammoth cost of this rarest of birds acoustic guitar.

This guitar features many of millionth Martin guitar's audacious and downright lavish inlays with select pearl on its back, pick guard, headplate, fingerboard and bridge. Herringbone pearl inlay encircles the top, and the rosette features the same herringbone pearl inlay, flanked by two pearl rings in select abalone. The neck and headstock are not left out of the fray, as they feature borders inlaid in select pearl. Somewhere, a cash register is salivating.

The D-100 Deluxe is crafted with Adirondack Spruce and C.I.T.E.S. certified Brazilian rosewood, hand selected specifically for this edition. Golden Era amenities like scalloped 5/16" Adirondack spruce top braces, a 1 3/4" modified V neck with square, tapered headstock and diamond volute all elbow for the main stage with signature touches like Waverly gold hand-engraved tuners with butterbean knobs, gold color frets and fossilized ivory bridge and end pins topped with green tourmaline dots in 14-karat gold settings. The nut and saddle are fashioned from fossilized ivory.

Each D-100 Deluxe guitar in the edition of 50 bears a custom printed interior label personally signed by Martin Chairman C.F. Martin IV and is numbered in sequence. In keeping with the instrument's exalted place as the Martin model with the most precious additions ever, the D-100 Deluxe is presented to the well-appointed purchaser in a special black five-ply case covered in genuine leather and fitted with a black crushed velour interior.

Martin's Guitar Innovations

The Martin Company is generally credited with developing the X-bracing system, during the 1850s. Unfortunately (or perhaps, fortunately), C. F. Martin did not apply for a patent on the new bracing system. During the 1850s, X-bracing was used by several makers, all German immigrants who knew each other, and according to historian Philip Gura, there is no evidence that C.F. Martin invented the system. The Martin guitar company was the first to use X-bracing on a large scale, however, and Martin has gone on record as claiming to be the inventor of the "scalloped X-bracing" system of construction as well.

Martin's popularity continued to grow into the 1900s, due to the rise of country & western music as well as the continued drive of folk. Country music demanded a louder instrument, and many companies began to shift from an instrument whose strings were made from catgut, to those of steel. C.F Martin & Co began moving their focus to this type of acoustic guitar by the very early 1920s.

Opposite page: a closer look at the Martin D-100 Deluxe

Martin

OM-42 Cambodian Rosewood

For every number one, there is a number two. This guitar is barely eclipsed by the D-100 in price range, and while there are those that would argue the need for such a high ticket item, no one seems to doubt that Martin would be the ideal acoustic guitar company to do it.

The Martin OM-42 Cambodian Rosewood Acoustic is an extremely limited run guitar, with a total of only 30 being produced. Scarcity breeds demand. This instrument features an Adirondack red spruce top, and solid Cambodian rosewood back and sides. The OM-42 guitar also features a genuine mahogany neck fitted to the body with a dovetail joint, and 1/4" standard, scalloped Adirondack spruce bracing for improved tonal clarity. Grained ivoroid binding and select abalone and pearl inlays are the summit for this 2nd place finisher in the race to see who can fell more rare/ endangered trees in the name of craft and rarified tone. These two guitars would pale in price comparison to the millionth produced, however, as it was encrusted with rubies and other precious stones.

Martin Guitars and Rock & Roll

In the late 1960s, Martin manufactured hollow-body electric guitars similar to those manufactured by Gretsch. Martin's electric guitars were not popular (seldom seen by musicians) and the company then decided to continue to concentrate on the manufacture of a wide range of high quality acoustics. They also brought back the famous (and more expensive) D-45 in 1968.

During the 1960s, many musicians preferred Martin guitars built before World War II to the more recent guitars of the same model. The pre-war guitars were believed to have internal bracing carved more skillfully than the later instruments, producing better resonance. Additionally, the 1960s Martin dreadnoughts suffered from poor intonation in the higher registers. This is attributed by some luthiers and repairmen to a gradual trend of misplacing the bridge on these guitars. Apparently, the same jigs for bridge placement were used throughout the history of each model's production. As the amount of production increased from the Martin factory, the jigs eroded, resulting in inaccurate bridge placement. This was eventually identified and corrected, though not before Martin had already produced a wealth of de-valued acoustic instruments. In 1979 Martin opened their custom shop that saw the creation of their 500,000th guitar in 1990, the millionth being created fourteen years later in 2004.

Although Martin continued to make their complete range of acoustic guitar models and continually added innovations, musicians preferred the vintage models, and they gladly paid premium prices for "Golden Era" Martins. That Martin has the ability to create the industry's most expensive instruments is a testament to their success and reputation as the pinnacle of guitar making. From the very beginning, Martin has had very little in the way of "competition" for its throne, though many have tried and in the process garnered strong followings, but none with the instant awe and star power of C.F Martin & Co.

Opposite Page: a closer look at the Martin OM-42 Cambodian Rosewood guitar

Martin

000-18 Golden Era 1937 Sunburst

The Martin Marquis 000-18 Sunburst Acoustic Guitar is a more affordable vintage Martin recreation of the Golden Era 1937 original. Marquis guitars feature Golden Era fixtures but utilize East Indian Rosewood backs, sides, and head plates. The modern interpretation also has Adirondack Spruce and late game improvements such as adjustable truss rods and modified v-shape necks. While this does not qualify as a true "starter instrument" for the acoustic guitar player, it does represent a classic piece of the Martin style of production, and while corners have been cut to keep the price in check, quality and tone remain.

The Martin Dreadnought Body Style

Martin's greatest innovation in the field of guitar making of the period 1915-1930 was the dreadnought guitar. Today it is as ubiquitously used as the X-bracing method of construction. Originally devised in 1916 as a collaborative effort between Martin and a prominent retailer, the Oliver Ditson Co., the dreadnought body style was larger and deeper than most guitars. In 1906, the Royal Navy had shocked the world by launching a battleship that was considerably larger than any in service. From the idea that a ship that big would have to fear nothing, it was christened HMS Dreadnought. The saying among sailors of that time was, "fear God, and Dreadnought." That is, until the battleship was eventually scuttled.

Martin recognized a perfect marketing tie-in when they saw one, and borrowed the name for their new, large guitar. The greater volume and louder bass produced by this expansion in size was intended to make the guitar more useful as an accompaniment instrument for singers working with the limited sound equipment of the day. Initial models for Ditson were fan-braced, and the instruments were poorly received. Fan-braced acoustic guitars lacked the ability to sustain and survive the vibration and deep resonance that the dreadnought body style created.

In 1931, Martin reintroduced the style with a modified body shape to accommodate a 14-fret neck, and it quickly became their best-selling guitar. The rest of the industry soon followed, and today the "dreadnought" size and shape is considered one of the "standard" acoustic guitar shapes, iconic for its use in a wide variety of musical genres.

Martin also developed a line of arch-top instruments during the 1930s. Their design differed from Gibson and other arch-tops in a variety of respects - the fingerboard was glued to the top, rather than a floating extension of the neck, and the backs and sides were flat rosewood plates pressed into an arch rather than the more common carved figured maple. Martin arch-tops were not commercially successful and were withdrawn after several years. In spite of this, during the 1960s, David Bromberg had a Martin arch-top converted to a flat-top guitar with exceptionally successful results, and as a result, Martin began issuing a David Bromberg model based on this conversion.

During this time, Martin also continued to make ukuleles, and other stringed instruments, many of which survive in excellent condition to the present day and are prized by collectors as well as musicians.

Opposite page: a closer look at the Martin 000-18 Sunburst Guitar

Martin

00-28VS

The Martin 00-28VS recreates a pre-World War II acoustic guitar that features a solid Sitka spruce top, solid East Indian rosewood back and sides, and a select hardwood modified V-shaped neck. The 00-28VS guitar's appointments include black and white boltaron endpiece and back inlays, zig-zag back purfling, a grained ivoroid heelcap, and diamond and square fingerboard position inlays. This comfortable Martin guitar produces a remarkably rich depth of tone, with clear trebles that are not overshadowed by the bass notes.

Martin and the Modeling Numbers

For many years, Martin has used a model-labeling system that consists of an initial letter or a number or series of zeros that specifies the body size and type (5 being the smallest and J being the largest) followed by a number that designates the guitar's ornamentation and style, including the species of wood from which the guitar is constructed. In general, the higher the acoustic guitars' serial number, the higher the level of ornamentation on the guitar itself. Additional letters or numbers added to this basic system are used to designate special features (such as a built-in pickup or a cutaway).

Martin also periodically offers special models. Many of these have a limited production run, or begin as a limited-production guitar that sells well enough to become regularly produced. Many of these special models are designed with, endorsed by, and named after well-known guitarists such as Eric Clapton, Merle Haggard, Stephen Stills, Paul Simon, Arlo Guthrie, Johnny Cash (described herein), and many others. In 1997, Martin launched its "Women in Music" series which then was followed in 1998 by the Joan Baez Signature guitar, a replica of the 0-45 with which Baez began her career. We have examined a few of these "limited run" acoustic instruments as they describe the very finest in craftsmanship and represent (arguably) the pinnacle of tradition melded with modern luthiering and ideas.

Opposite page: Joan Baez, playing a Martin 00-28VS acoustic live in 1970

Other Instruments of Note

Dominic Frasca, a classically-trained guitar virtuoso, created a 10-string guitar by grafting the neck from an electric guitar onto a Martin Millennium (a nylon string acoustic originally crafted by Thomas Humphrey) acoustic guitar. He also added single string "mini capos" which form part of his trademark style and sound.

Roger McGuinn worked with C. F. Martin & Company to develop a seven-string folk guitar. McGuinn's guitar, the D7, is tuned in the same manner as a standard folk guitar with steel strings, but the third (G) string is augmented with a harmonic string one octave higher. The intention was to afford the six-string player the chance to play "jangly" twelve-string style lead guitar.

By the modern era, C.F Martin & Co were (and still are) producing over 180 unique models of acoustic guitar. With their success cemented, Martin has looked to continue in the vein of their initial desire: quality. Nothing is more proof of that desire than the fact that the location of Martin's workshop remains where it began: Nazareth, Pennsylvania.

Martin

Steel String Backpacker Guitar

Cheap. Diminutive. Well traveled. The backpacker is a no frills model from the C.F Martin guitar company that allows the player to be anywhere while still being able to satisfy the need to play. A braced, solid tonewood top with a solid mahogany neck, back, and sides gives this interestingly-shaped acoustic guitar a surprisingly high level of resonance and projection. The Backpacker was built to withstand the rigors of camping, hiking, and off-road traveling. It includes high quality chrome-enclosed tuners. A unique bridge on the nylon-string version accepts either plain or ball-end classic strings. All of this (and more), and the instrument weighs less than 2-1/2 lbs. There are those that have said the Backpacker is more difficult to play than a regular-sized acoustic body but we would expect that to be the case: it is the size of a toddler. That being said the guitar does a great job at being an ambassador for Martin, putting the company's face in locales that otherwise would not see it.

C.F Martin and the Disappearing Trees

Due to deforestation and intensive wood use, both in the guitar industry and others, wood is increasingly rare. The quality timber that luthiers seek to build premium, frontline instruments dwindles by the day, and makes the search for sustainable materials all the more important. Some companies have sought synthetic solutions, choosing lighter polymers or allowing electronics to play a larger role in their guitar manufacturing. Martin enacted a program in the very early 1990s that was aimed at creating sustainable timber use, and seeking alternative tone woods outside of the traditional mahogany, spruce, and rosewood. Their aim is to educate the rest of the industry on creating resources that are renewable, and cause less harm during the creation of wonderful acoustic instruments. The company's own research has shown that the modern acoustic guitar player would prefer a guitar with cosmetic imperfections caused by woods in their natural states over the strip mining of accepted "industry accepted" species. The company recognizes CITES as the governing authority on endangered species and closely follows their directives.

Martin is using their industry clout in a way that other companies have not, and that is to lead by example using honest business practices, rather than raw profit and sales numbers (even though Martin has those as well). The acoustic guitar industry is well aware that the consumer pays attention to C.F Martin & Co., and will (in general) agree with their principles because of Martin's long reputation for high quality. Simply put, if Martin does it, the rest of the companies had better follow suit or risk being left behind, something that, in this fiercely competitive field, no one can afford to have happen to them.

Why Are They So Expensive?

A guitar's cost is determined by a number of factors: the production methods (factory vs. workshop), the woods used in its creation, its electronics (if any), and the quantity produced. Martin guitars have a rare combination of optimal conditions in nearly every category. Almost all instruments are produced in the United States, with premium materials, and many on limited production runs. It ensures a unique experience for every musician, and guarantees that they will never regret a Martin guitar purchase.

Opposite page: a closer look at the Martin Steel String Backpacker guitar

X Series: DCXE BLACK

The Martin DCXE Cutaway Acoustic Electric Guitar features an easy-playing cutaway dreadnought body equipped with a Fishman pickup and Prefix Pro EQ. The low-oval profile Stratabond (laminated plywood) neck has a black 12" radius Micarta fingerboard with side dots only and jumbo frets to provide greater ease of hammer-ons, pull-offs, and bends. 1-11/16" nut, 25-3/8" scale. Series specific features include a black peghead overlay with gold logo, enclosed chrome tuners, and a strap button. The X series provides many features that are available on more expensive Martin guitars, but in a more cost effective manner. The black finish on the guitar is eye catching, and also serves as a reminder of the history of Martin guitars, and their reluctance to use such finishes orginally. The use of stratabond in particular offers a means for the guitar maker to shave a corner while still maintaining the integrity of the product. Electronics play a role as well, with preamps and pickups allowing for less woodworking.

How Non-Rockstars Cope

For the everyday guitar player, an elite instrument is a figment of the imagination; a dream through paned glass or a brief encounter at a guitar shop. The lack of fame and fortune leads them to be bridesmaids only, suffering with mediocre instruments. Martin is one of many companies that have heard the cries from guitar players around the world, and with their X Series, join guitar manufacturers like Epiphone and Fender in the creation of a line that is pocketbook friendly. Who knows, maybe the penniless player that manages to put one of these guitars in their hands could ride to fame and greater fortune, thereby increasing Martin's reputation in the music world at large. Anything is possible.

Rock and roll, fame and fortune aside, the X series competes very well with other comparable models from other guitar companies. While this is not entirely surprising, it is somewhat uncommon for a guitar company sporting models with six figure price tags to create a model for under a thousand dollars and with such care as to not skimp on the instrument's tone and durability. The true test of any guitar company as we move into an age where digital media makes every bit of information instantly accessible, and competition for consumer attention is at its greatest, is the task to remain relevant, remain a company that is viewed with modern eyes, not just those of the past or the "Golden Era." Honoring the past and preserving the methods of those master luthiers and the models they created is absolutely essential, but to view them as the pinnacle of guitar production is just as important as innovation and the confidence of the guitar player. How the acoustic has endured is riding that razor's edge of tradition and innovation. From Luna guitars to Gibson to Martin, each company keeps its traditions and works from that solid

Opposite page: a closer look at the Martin DCXE Black guitar

Martin

Special Edition: POW MIA

The POW MIA Dreadnought Special Edition Acoustic Guitar was designed by a small group of Martin employees to honor the families of American servicemen and women who were held captive or are still missing in action. A stainless steel bracelet will be sent to the original owner upon completion of the Martin warranty. A portion of the proceeds from the sale of each POW MIA guitar will be donated to the National Alliance of Families for the return of America's missing servicemen and women.

The guitar is a dreadnought-sized body of mahogany and Sitka spruce, finished entirely in black with a single ring of abalone at the soundhole. White body binding is bordered on top, sides, & back with layered black/white lines. The peghead has a silver Martin detail with the POW MIA flag below it and the slogan "You Are Not Forgotten". The ebony fretboard has a pearl flag and eagle inlaid at the first fret (designed as a special tribute to former Martin employee and Marine Corps veteran Barry Rinker by his son), large pearl letters spelling POW MIA from the 3rd through 9th frets, teardrops at 12,15, & 17 and a pearl version of the Prisoner of War Ribbon at the 19 fret. Inside the guitar is a label signed by C.F. Martin IV and the neck block is engraved to read "POW*MIA All Gave Some, Some Gave All". Upon registering the warranty with the Martin Co, the owner will receive a stainless steel bracelet (mentioned above) engraved "UNTIL THEY ALL COME HOME" C.F. MARTIN & CO., INC. Other features include: modified low oval neck (25.4" scale, 1-11/16" nut), hybrid scalloped braces, black pickguard, ebony belly bridge, black bridgepins with abalone dots, chrome enclosed tuning gears, black nut & saddle. Geib style case has black hardware and plush American flag lining in the lid.

Guitars as a Means of Charity

Here we see the powerful message that the guitar is able to send. Guitar companies have often used their instruments in charity work, silent auctions and the like, though none with perhaps as powerful a message as Martin's. It is both commendable and honorable to see a guitar company use its fame and industry credibility to create an instrument for such a wonderful cause. There are other companies doing similar things: Godin has long made contributions to the Montreal Jazz Festival, and Daisy Rock continually supports young girl's music camps.

Music is a timeless necessity. It permeates through cultures, religions, and economic status. The guitar has become the defining instrument of the American tradition; its companies are a mirror of the independent spirit that birthed it many years ago. The guitar company as a charitable organization makes perfect sense. Musicians come from diverse backgrounds of all walks of life and many leave behind poor neighborhoods on their way to fame and fortune. It is comforting to see that Martin is not forgetting anyone.

Ditson Dreadnought 111

Like the original 1916 model, the Ditson Dreadnought 111 Acoustic Guitar features mahogany back and sides, an Adirondack spruce top, Brazilian rosewood head plate and binding, ebony pyramid bridge, ebony fingerboard with graduated position markers at the 5th, 7th, and 9th, frets and a 1-7/8" nut width. The exact details of Ditson's unique single ring wood rosette have been recreated. Special three-in-line Waverly tuners on the slotted headstock are true to the original look and feel. The original "Oliver Ditson Co., Boston, New York" stamp created in 1916 was retrieved from the Martin archives and used on the back of the headstock and center strip inside the guitar.

Martin designed this original dreadnought for Oliver Ditson in the early 1900s and it was the first of its body type ever to be created. Thought by some to be too large and too "loud" to be an effective acoustic instrument, the dreadnought would go on (in spite of early criticism) to be the most popular guitar of its (or any other) day.

The Continuing Work

Martin has been a pioneer in the field of acoustic guitars for many years. They are purported to have invented the X-bracing system, increased the length of the fretboard from 12 frets to 14, and created a body style that defined generations of musicians and songwriters. To many, C.F Martin & Co. is peerless. There are many guitar companies that have created great and useful innovations from Martin's original designs and used them very well - none, however, matches the original.

With industry leading initiatives in sustainable growth, significant charity work, and a product line that is a perennial attention-getter, the task for Martin is to maintain speed at this date in history. Martin as a company is proof that the march of time may not trump true craftsmanship and quality materials, and this is seen most admirably in the reissue of the Ditson Dreadnought. This acoustic guitar is a look into the past with a modern eye, to see where the company came from, and what modern amenities may be employed in the craft of an instrument that has been so important to the industry as a whole.

Still headed by members of the Martin family, the company now looks to change the industry mindset regarding manufacturing locations and production methods. It will be interesting to see if Martin can be as successful in this area of the market as they have been in selling guitars to the public. It will be an important decision however, as supplies of these already rare and expensive materials continue to dwindle by the moment, and not just as a result of guitar makers. These woods are prized in the making of furniture, ornate jewelry and other musical instruments. While some may argue that this is not the acoustic guitar industry's problem to solve, it is someone's, and what better place to start than with the organizations that are already doing good work in their founding communities.

Opposite page,: a closer look at Martin Ditson Dreadnought 111

00 Concert Model

Bil Mitchell began making acoustic guitars in 1979. He produces them in the same shop where he started nearly thirty years ago in Bucks County, Pennsylvania, and has no affiliation with the import line of "Mitchell" guitars. What separates his guitars from the rest? Mitchell's extensive ability in all aspects of guitar construction - from engineering, to unique artistic expression, and this is what easily puts him in an elite category of independent luthiers. If scarcity breeds demand, Mitchell will need to be a one man army.

Exceptional tone woods are not the entirety of Mitchell's appeal. Six available body sizes, custom neck widths, bridge styles, headstock, and scale lengths create the custom palette for a rainbow of hand cut mother of pearl, abalone, river pearl, and ivory inlays, designed and executed by Bil himself. It is encouraging to see an independent luthier thriving in an industry so dominated by large corporations or top-notch workshops with hundreds of years as a head start.

Bil Mitchell, and repair expert Sarah Dieterichs own and operate the Guitar Parlor: a joint effort of these two masters. They are located in Eastern Pennsylvania on the Delaware River, in the northernmost tip of Bucks County (30 miles north of Philadelphia). They are not very far from where C.F Martin moved his groundbreaking workshop in the late 1800s.

They have more capabilities and experience within their walls then the average guitar player might expect. Not only do they handcraft Bil Mitchell Custom Guitars and Homegrown Guitars, they also perform extensive repairs on all stringed instruments ranging from basic set-ups to complete restorations, with extreme care attention. The focus of their business is one that is familiar and synonymous with all great companies that begin very humbly: "create quality instruments for the musician, and they will be yours for life."

The Concert Model

This acoustic is slightly larger than the Parlor style model, which will be discussed later. It sports a classic era fretboard length at 12 frets at 14" wide at the lower bout and 39" overall. The concert model produces a very mellow tone and surprising resonance for something its size which is a testament to Mitchell's fine skill as a luthier.

Mitchell's skill is right in the open with his series of acoustic guitars. His place in history is an important one at is shows how modern independent shops are surviving in rough economic times. The master luthier does an excellent job of explaining his process, how he goes about crafting his unique instruments from the very first stages on up to the finished product. It is a rare look inside an artists' studio and one that Mitchell does not shy away from. His seeming openness and air of honesty about the love of his craft is what is missing from a larger, faceless company that has removed itself from the ground level art form of crafting fine instruments in the face of marketing strategies and selling points.

Opposite page: Mitchell 00 series Concert Model guitar

Above: Guitarist Kasim Sulton (centre) is one of many artist who uses a Bil Mitchell guitar. From left to right: Prairie Prince, Elliot Easton, Kasim Sulton, Todd Rundgren and Greg Hawkes of 'The New Cars' at the House of Blues in West Hollywood.
Opposite page: The 000 style is a perfect compliment to the Orchestra model

Orchestra Model

This model of acoustic guitar was created for the player that requires a greater range of tonal response. The guitar boasts a longer fretboard at 14 frets with Mitchell's own unique style Maple-bound ebony bridge. Features include only the highest quality tonewoods available including an Ebony fingerboard and aforementioned bridge. All wood binding accents the headstock, fingerboard, bridge, and body. The main X brace of these guitars is laminated with carbon fiber for maximum stability and tonal response. Highly polished bone nut and saddle are standard, as is the high gloss nitrocellulose lacquer, buffed to an incredible sheen to accentuate the character of the woods.

Competing with the Big Ones

For the small company, producing fine instruments in a field where there are so many well established industry veterans can be intimidating. A guitar company like a Gibson or Fender already has the infrastructure in place to ship instruments around the world, build models quickly and capitalize on trends while they are at their highest profit potential. Bil Mitchell has kept right on building acoustic guitars under the veritable nose of the industry for nearly thirty years. How does he stay afloat?

It is not by charging exorbitant prices for his instruments. Most of Mitchell's handcrafted acoustic guitars are priced on par with a comparable acoustic built by the larger Martin Guitar Company. This small shop is following the same path as the large workshops did many years ago. That is, Bil Mitchell is building relationships with artists, staying steadfast in his love of producing consistent instruments, and keeping the product in the hands of the musicians. We have talked about the history of guitar companies, how they "got their start" and here we see it happening live, in our time, which is exciting.

Homegrown guitars, Mitchell's production imprint, has also been seen for purchase on several online retailers in addition to the luthier's own workshop. The combination of modern internet-savvy selling strategies and excellent product are what help the smaller guitar builders to post a profit even with a production staff of just two: Mitchell and Dieterichs. The smaller production staff and lack of any real electronics attachments precludes Mitchell to producing "Golden Era" style instruments, though that doesn't seem to be a problem for the luthier. His workshop's homepage is covered with thank you messages and high praise for his instruments. "One day, while looking for a special guitar I stopped in at Bucks county folk music shop where I played several nice, high end guitars," writes Steve Begley, "Karl finally handed me a guitar you built. This was a guitar that actually sang! And the way it played was a joy, the guitar felt like it played itself. I continued my search when I realized that every other guitar I played was being compared to yours, your guitar became the touchstone of everything I played. I went back and purchased the guitar and have not regretted it for a moment! With your guitar there is a certain "old world" craftsmanship that is evident in the perfect joints, in the finish, in the inlays, in everything. The guitar is exquisite to look at, wonderful to listen to, and a joy to play!"

The Parlor

The parlor is the smallest of the Mitchell designs, with a 12-fret neck, pyramid bridge, and slotted headstock. The term "parlor guitar" dates back to the days before recorded music where entertainment was conducted live and often in the parlors of those who were lucky enough to have them.

Today, the term describes a size and style of guitar. Parlor guitars have smaller bodies than dreadnoughts and often are smaller than even classical guitars. The intent of the instrument's creation with a reduced size is not to accommodate smaller guitar player, but rather to provide for a more even frequency response. In other words, bass, treble and all of the frequencies in between are the same volume. In an acoustically near perfect environment like a "parlor" or concert hall, this even frequency response is a must if the music isn't to be overwhelmed with bass.

Often (in fact, usually), the neck of a parlor guitar is wider than that of a dreadnought. Parlor guitars are often the choice of fingerstyle players. The wider neck better accommodates this style of player giving him/her more room to get individual fingers between the strings. Anyone looking for a guitar would be well served to consider a good parlor style guitar. The mid frequencies of these guitars are punchy and pleasing, making these instruments a good choice for all but the classical or flamenco player.

Having a Place at the Table

The testimonials from happy guitar players continue to roll in for Bil Mitchell and his homegrown line of acoustics. "I have played guitar since 1960 and owned many different instruments; Gibson, Martin, Breedlove, Robertson and LoPrinzi to name a few," writes Ron Harkov, "I have never experienced the combination of impeccable workmanship, beautiful woods, easy playability and great tone as I have with both my Cherry and Maple Homegrowns. What can I say? Anyone I meet that wants a great small body guitar I will tell them to check out the folks at the Guitar Parlor. Thanks for making me a pair of awesome instruments!"

All of this street credibility builds momentum for Mitchell and his small team who have faithfully adhered to their company message of keeping the customer first and foremost. What is also appealing about Mitchell's shop is his ability to give each guitar player the feeling that they have walked away with a truly customized instrument made just for them – because that's exactly what they have; a unique instrument built to their specifications in the same way that Gibson or Martin have gone to famous guitar players throughout the years. Mitchell has done for the everyday player at a price that they can afford.

That is not to say that Homegrown guitars are only played by the common man. Mitchell's creations have their found their way into the hands of Greg Lipsky of Grace Potter's Nocturnals and Glen Burtnik, who has recorded songs for such artists as Don Henley and country music star Randy Travis.

Opposite page: Glen Burtnik of The Beatles tribute band Liverpool performs at the Fest for Beatles Fans 2007 at the Mirage Hotel & Casino on July 1, 2007 in Las Vegas, Nevada.

2009 Collector's Edition Koa Acoustic-Electric

This latest collector's edition from Ovation is an example of marketing instruments to the musician as a collector's item. It features a hand-selected top of figured koa, which creates warm, full-bodied tone that belies Ovation's space-aged design. The guitar is very lightweight (a featured characteristic of Ovation designs) with its single cutaway contoured body it is highly ergonomic for the player. Bells and whistles include a specially designed abalone Celtic knot rosette and fingerboard inlays add to the aesthetic appeal of the instrument and show that the luthiers spared no expense in crafting this collector's edition. There are over 200 individually laid abalone sections that surround the Koa's top.

Powering the electric side is Ovation's OP Pro Studio preamp featuring exclusive "expressor"/drive controls that accentuate single note passages or each individual note when playing finger style. It has been developed to work specifically with the unique Ovation Patented Pickup; this professional grade system has been engineered to compliment the unique character of Ovation guitars. It provides the guitar player with that essential "plugged-in" sound and offers a range of features that will enhance any musician's performance in any venue. As the next design in the OP-Pro series, it offers the same great sound as the OP-Pro but also features a unique analog signal processor Ovation called an "Expressor" (as mentioned above) that brings new versatility to plugged-in performances. Ovation has created but 150 of these models, which will no doubt, add to the fervor of collectors and discerning musicians to pick one up

Collector's Edition Wood Choices

Even with the "collector's edition" tag attached to the Koa, Ovation is still able (through the crafting methods and materials in their building) to offer the instrument at a price far below what industry expectations for a "collector's edition" would be. Its wood selection is of interesting to note as Ovation guitars do not use wood for their bodies they were able to choose a higher grade for its top. Koa is native to the Hawaiian Islands where it was used by natives for canoes and surfboards. Koa's usage as a tonewood in acoustic guitar construction is one that must be held in check, and moderated as it takes 20 to 25 years of growth to generate a tree that is of a useful size to the luthier.

Above: Ray Davies performing live onstage, playing an Ovation acoustic guitar

Celebrity Deluxe Double

Two guitars for the price of…two. The newly designed acoustic/electric features a twelve string neck on top and six string on the bottom with a toggle switch that allows players to select six string-on, twelve string-on, or both-on at the same time through a modified OP24+ preamp. To balance it out, Ovation has developed a new super shallow size roundback body that is specifically designed for this instrument and makes it surprisingly comfortable to play. The necks are full-scale 25" length. The history of the deluxe double is one full of rock and roll pomp and stage presence. Its electric counterparts, popularized by Jimmy Page, are the stuff of lore and legend.

A Unique Look for the Acoustic

Ovation as a guitar company has pioneered a new slant in the production of their acoustic guitars. It began in 1966, when aeronautical frontrunner Charlie Kaman unexpectedly revolutionized the instrument. As a longtime guitarist, he understood the needs of players and his extensive helicopter blade experience gave him a rare understanding of vibration that most luthiers and guitar manufacturers rarely come across.

Kaman believed he possessed the technology and the know-how to truly create a better acoustic guitar. In 1964, Charlie gathered a small team of aerospace engineers (yes engineers) and set to work improving the instrument. These men were scientists, and went about the problem as men of that ilk would: identifying the issues, and researching and solving the problem in a very methodical way. They discovered that the flat back of an acoustic guitar actually hindered the balance and projection. So, these engineers started breaking the time honored traditions of acoustic guitar construction. Instead of the flat-top or the arch-top, Ovation was the first to create the round-back guitar. Their guitar improved the projection qualities of the instrument, bettered its resonance and balance, as well giving it a sleeker, more modern look. Two years later the first Ovation rumbled off the production line: The Balladeer.

Realities of the Invention

So-called "flat-backed" acoustic guitars are still the industry standard, though Ovation has carved out a significant portion of the market share with its round-backed acoustics. The polymers used in their creation are in stark contrast to the all wooden construction of the traditional acoustic instruments, and present an interesting solution to the shrinking pool of natural materials that go into guitar manufacturing. Kaman, founder of Ovation, held a widely accounted distaste for natural components in guitar creation such as animal hair and glue. In fact, Ovation's birth was generated from a failed attempt by Kaman to purchase the C.F Martin guitar company when Kaman took his then Martin acoustic to their workshop to have it repaired, and discovered their luthiers still using animal glue and hammers.

Martin refused. Kaman returned a second time bringing his plans for the future of the acoustic guitar with him. Martin refused a second time and the wheels that would see what would be Ovation guitars on the market were set into motion.

Above: Julian Cope performing live onstage, playing an Ovation acoustic guitar

Ovation

Custom Legend

The Custom Legend represents the top-of-the line models within the Ovation line-up, using the highest quality materials to produce outstanding sound. The tops of these instruments are marked by their unrivaled flexibility and are among the best on the market today. No fewer than 300 individual pieces of the finest abalone have been hand-inlaid by experienced workers, and serve as a perfect example of the skilled craftsmanship of the Ovation luthiers.

The Ovation Elite has been given a full upgrade to create the C2078 LX acoustic-electric guitar. It's lighter, louder, richer and fuller; all qualities that are desirable for the acoustic guitar player of today. C2078 LX innovations include: a lightweight dual-action truss rod makes precision adjustments simple. Carbon fiber stabilizers keep the fingerboard perfectly aligned at the neck/body joint. The exotic wood leaf-shaped "epaulets" are now inlaid into the top with laser precision. The new cleaner design actually offers a slight sound enhancement. Play a new LX and prepare to be impressed by the hugeness of the acoustic sound.

The Legend possesses deeper, richer sound, coupled with the legendary Ovation balance and clarity. The smooth, hard composite Lyrachord GS body improves projection and reflects top vibrations better than traditional material and is now even lighter and stronger. Six separate elements sense both string and top vibration, giving each player a better string-to-string balance, no matter what string type or gauge is in use. Designed in collaboration with Al DiMeola and Melissa Etheridge, the new Op-Pro Preamp is voiced to give the Legend an arena-sized sound with a minimal strain or stress. Every improvement comes directly from the needs of pro players and sound engineers.

Ovation's Custom Legend is also built from the choicest top woods. These AAA-graded tops are the most flexible and consistent Sitka spruce tops available. Only 5% of all Ovation's graded tops are chosen for these fine instruments. Artistry is also something to consider with the Custom as well, as over 300 individual pieces of abalone shell are hand-inlaid into each Custom Legend, a stunning appearance in any finish.

Wide Ranging Appeal

Ovation has enjoyed a wide array of artist appeal since its creation in the 1960s. Many musicians, both famous and otherwise, have been attracted to the company's unique body style and customizable amenities. Melissa Etheridge has been a long time Ovation player, though there are recent newcomers to the family. Mick Thompson of Slipknot also has his own Custom MT37, designed in collaboration with the Ovation team to withstand Slipknot's battlefield-like live shows.

In an industry with long running standards of tradition, and a sense of "time honored methods" Ovation has come along exactly when the market needs it most. They are company that is producing instruments that appear truly "futuristic," and stand in stark contrast to the instruments being produced by the likes of Martin, Fender, and Gibson. The polymers used in construction also serve to keep Ovation's cost to the consumer relatively low when compared to the solid wood acoustics of their competitors.

Opposite page: a closer look at the Ovation Custom Legend

Ovation

Above: Singer Neil Diamond performs onstage with an Ovation acoustic guitar in circa 1977 in Los Angeles, California
Opposite page: Ovation iDea acoustic guitar

Standard Balladeer

It's the guitar that started the journey of a revolutionary body design. The Ovation Standard Balladeer 1771 AX is a 6-string acoustic electric guitar with a mid-depth body and an AA solid Spruce top. The 1771 AX features scalloped X-bracing, a Rosewood fretboard and bridge, chrome tuning machines, and a pearl Oak leaf rosette. The onboard Ovation OCP-1K pickup delivers classic Ovation tone for the guitarist that demands a great plug-in experience.

The preamp is the story of the new Balladeer which was produced in cooperation with some of music's finest guitar players. The new OP-PRO combines state of the art audio quality with guitarist-friendly features for a preamp that should please even the most discriminating player. Developed to work specifically with the unique Ovation Patented Pickup, this professional grade system has been engineered to compliment the unique character of Ovation guitars. It provides the individual player with that essential "plugged-in" sound, and offers a range of features that will enhance performance in any venue. As the next design in the OP-Pro series, it offers the same signature sound as the OP-Pro but also features a unique analog signal processor that Ovation has dubbed the "Expressor", because it brings new versatility to the acoustic guitar player's plugged-in performances.

The Newest iDEA in Acoustic Guitar

When the Ovation guitar was introduced in 1966, recording studios occupied entire buildings. In 2008, Ovation introduced an entirely new piece of technology for the acoustic guitar. The Ovation iDea is the first and only guitar of its kind, featuring a built-in MP3 recorder/player. The digital recorder is part of the on-board Ovation preamp. The patented technology makes possible a list of features never before available on any guitar, acoustic or electric. From the company with a signature feel for the coming age of the acoustic guitar, comes more smart business practices. Imagine where we would be if C.F Martin had thought to patent the X-brace?

Songwriters have always desired a simple and convenient way to record song ideas, hooks, melodies and lyrics. With the iDea, players who write on guitar will have an instantly accessible high-quality digital recorder with them wherever they go. The simple and direct recording control makes it easy to record entire songs or fragments, even vocals and commentary. The iDea can record from the guitar alone, simultaneously from the guitar and built-in microphone, and from an auxiliary input. Any audio signal fed into the auxiliary input is converted to an MP3 file and stored in the iDea memory. The iDea is also a learning tool, with audio lessons pre-installed in the memory. Additional lessons from iDea educational partner, WorkshopLive.com, will be available via download.

Guitarists who enjoy jamming will find a tireless band mate in the iDea. Several "Jam Tracks" are pre-installed in the instrument, and others are available online. Downloading files from a computer or the Internet is easy via USB. Files in the iDea can be moved, renamed, deleted and rearranged right on the computer desktop. Mixes from recording software, rhythm tracks, even songs the player wants to learn can be downloaded and played either through the guitar output or headphones.

Adamas

Introduced in 1976, the Adamas is still one of the most advanced acoustic guitars ever produced. The Adamas was born out of the same spirit of innovation that developed Ovation's signature Roundback.

Adamas is the Latin word for diamond in its native form, carbon. Kaman Aerospace used carbon fiber in components for satellites and supersonic aircrafts, and used this material in the creation of Ovation's roundbacks. The team realized that carbon fiber, when heated, behaves much like wood, and they used this to their advantage. The Adamas top is made of aerospace-grade graphite in long fibers, designed to respond like Spruce. At one-third the weight of a Spruce top, the Adamas soundboard responds quicker, speaks louder and vibrates longer.

It's been just over 30 years since the first prototypes of the Adamas were seen in public. While there have been many improvements made over the years, the concept has proven itself. The Adamas still speaks just as loudly as the Balladeer as one of the most advanced acoustics on the market today, with a look that instantly recognizable.

Technology. Technology. Technology

Ovation's Adamas Premier blends both classic and brand new technology for a unique configuration of features. An ultra-light carbon fiber composite top, supported by the traditional Adamas "suspended ring", provides an extremely thin and responsive soundboard. Its 12-fret-to-body design and deep bowl also contribute to the Premier's big acoustic sound.

The Adamas 1680-NWT guitar, is equipped with Ovation's VIP, "Virtual Image Processing"- preamp which reproduces the same sound session players get playing into an industry quality microphone, in a sound proof booth. Now stunning, studio-quality acoustic performance can be taken to the stage or anywhere else players need superior acoustic electric performance.

Here we have seen, for the first time, a company take the improvements granted by the advance of science and implement them into the musical realm in a way that is readily accessible to the guitar player. These are not the province of producers or engineers working a large sound board, no, the Ovation line of guitars, illustrated in the Adamas line, is innovating on the fly.

The antithesis of traditionalism

Charlie Kaman dreamed a company that would build the better guitar. There are those that would argue that Ovation hasn't made the acoustic guitar better, but changed it into something else. The question that Ovation poses with its innovations and hardware additions is the definition of terms. How are we to define an acoustic instrument when vibration of the body and strings begins to matter less and less? It is true that the carbon which Ovation is using mimics wood in almost every aspect, but does it count? Are the purists ready to accept Ovation as a viable guitar company with a unique voice and a place in the world market? We would only have to look at the sales of their instruments to get the answer, and the fact that Ovation continues to sell well and appeal to perhaps the widest range of guitar players in the world would indicate a resounding 'yes'.

Opposite page: a closer look at an Adamas acoustic guitar
This page: Steve 'Luke' Lukather of Toto performs at The Music Mill on July 16, 2007 in Indianapolis, Indiana with his Adamas acoustic guitar

Elite

The USA made 1778T Elite T Acoustic-Electric Guitar from Ovation incorporates a simpler, untrimmed, 11-hole pattern that enhances the low and mid range punch. The Rock Maple neck profile has also been slimmed down to give it a look and feel more appealing to electric guitar players. An ultra light, yet incredibly durable, textured enamel finish is wrapped around the entire back and top.

The Elite T is outfitted with the new Ovation OP-30 preamp. Rich, bright and super quiet, the OP30 raises the bar in its class. Three bands of EQ plus the ability to shift the mid band to either a 450Hz or 970Hz gives you complete control over your sound. There's also a Pre-Shape circuit that not only lifts the bass and treble, but also reduces "rumble" from frequencies below 40Hz. And, as it is an Ovation, there's an on-board chromatic tuner.

The timeline going forward

Thirty years is not a lot of time when the life of other guitar companies are being considered. When compared to C.F Martin & Co., which has been in business for over 250 years, the company towers over the newborn Ovation. Where the upstart company makes up for its late arrival to the race is with spiffy tech. Ovation simply out-engineers their competition. Traditional acoustic guitar companies have called Ovation guitars "toys," looking down on their work as something for the less than serious musician, something to be experimented with, but not a lifelong commitment. If anything, Ovation has shrugged off these concerns with unwavering dedication to their craft that began from the refusal of one giant in the industry to see the technological light.

Opposite page: American singer, guitarist, and television host Glen Campbell adjusts a dial on his Ovation Deluxe acoustic - electric guitar

How Ovation Stole the Stage

Anyone that tuned into the "Glen Campbell Goodtime Hour" in the late 1960s saw Campbell playing an Ovation acoustic guitar. He approached Ovation to create an instrument that would allow him to step away from the microphone and continue playing - which was not possible at the time, given acoustic guitars' preamp requirements. Ovation studied existing models, and with the same fervor that had birthed the Balladeer a few years earlier, they created what would be regarded as the first acoustic/electric guitar ever made. In the early days of Ovation, it is estimated that only 15% of the guitars created had pickups, but by the 1970s that number had rocketed to 90%. That first pickup design is still in use in Ovation models that are created at the present time.

Ovation has maintained its leadership within the acoustic/electric market through a dogged desire to keep up with player needs. They have paid attention and worked closely when artists seek something more from an instrument or have questions regarding the equipment on current models. Their arm reaches a wide array of musicians, as we have seen from the grindcore of Slipknot, to the acoustic soul of Melissa Etheridge. The company that innovates stays alive. Even the larger guitar workshops are not immune to this trend, and it would seem that those who resist it are slowly falling by the wayside.

Parker

PA-28

Ken Parker began building and repairing guitars more than 25 years ago. Since that time, he has worked with countless musicians building instruments that further the definition of what the instrument can be, and what limits it can be stretched to. Parker Guitars was founded in the late 1990s, and quickly made a name for itself in the electric guitar field, only recently coming into its own with acoustics.

The Parker PA28 acoustic guitar has a folk-size body with a solid cedar top, solid rosewood back and an ebony fingerboard and bridge. Proprietarily unique Parker inlays adorn the fingerboard and a zero fret provides ideal string height. Choice woods and precise design provide full, balanced, articulate tone. Gold Grover 14:1 Sta-Tite tuners complete the look. Parker Intrigue Series guitars offer an innovative take on the traditional folk style. Unique features of the Intrigue Series acoustic guitars include an angled upper bout, an elliptic soundhole, and a bass balanced bridge. These guitars have a clean, bright, punchy folk style tone and are adorned with contemporary inlays and hardware; a rare combination of the traditional and unconventional.

Another Innovative New-Comer

Parker began his first workshop in Rochester, New York and produced several critically acclaimed guitar lines, but by 2003 he had sold the company in majority to the U.S. Music Corporation based in Illinois. The infusion of industry capital enabled Parker to open a custom guitar shop in 2005. Ken Parker returned to the company after what seems like a hiatus in 2006. He now produces only custom guitar models (to include his arch-tops project) for the company that still bears his name.

As a company, Parker is thought of as an innovator both stylistically and in terms of his craftsmanship. Parker guitars are just as easily recognizable as a Gibson, Martin, or Ovation. They have given Ibanez a serious run for their money in the "guitar for the virtuoso" category, as well by garnering the reputation of top-notch electronics and tone quality like no other 21st century guitar company.

Ken has created six new arch-top models for his "renewing the form" project. He has adjusted the soundholes on nearly all of the models, moving it clear off the top of the guitar towards the side and, as always, carrying the Parker signature headstock. The models are named - Olive Branch, Grace, Spot, Bubbles, and Mrs. Natural, and they look the part!

The challenge for Parker is breaking into the mainstream of acoustic guitar production. With a strong foothold already in the electric guitar world to enable the cross-over, Parker should be able to build on its early industry success and grow itself into a company with the power to stick around for many years to come. Their buyout nearly alienated their founder and chief creative force, though it appears that the ship has been righted, and Ken Parker is back, happy, and with creative juice left in the tank.

Opposite page: a closer look at the Parker PA-28 acoustic guitar

Parker

PA-24

Blonde is beautiful. This is no less true of Parker's PA-24, the acoustic that is the originator of the PA-28 and has that punchy folk sound. This guitar features a solid spruce top for wonderfully resonant intonation, birdseye maple back and sides, and an ivoroid fingerboard and bridge. Gold Grover 14:1 Sta-Tite tuners add to the guitar's overall appeal. A zero fret provides an industry standard in string height and ensures stable, balanced tones from open strings. Parker Intrigue Series guitars offer an innovative take on the traditional folk style. Unique features of the Intrigue Series acoustics include an angled upper bout, an elliptic soundhole, and bass balanced bridge.

The Advantages in Parker's Design

Parker has continually challenged traditional form with the guitars it has produced both in the electric and acoustic areas of production. They have used composite materials and resin over traditional tone woods and finishes, and where wood was necessary, Parker looked outside the traditional realm to Poplar and Basswood. They have also turned to using stainless steel frets as opposed to bone or other expensive materials (wood and nickel).

The guitar company has also worked to craft ergonomic guitars, ones that are more than easy access granters, but that are actually less strenuous to play. Many guitar players have reoccurring shoulder strain from nights on end of touring, or tendonitis from positioning fingers to pluck the right strings. It is great to see a company thinking about the instrument in a broader perspective, and one that may not have been so popular twenty years ago.

New Production Team

New production and design is currently led by Terry Atkins, of Gibson custom shop fame. Atkins has also worked with Tacoma Guitars, and Jackson. Terry has made several dynamic changes to the design of the flagship Fly (electric) model, all of which have increased the size and weight, including updating the truss rod, sacrificing the weight and the feel of the guitar, and diminishing the hands-on process to build these instruments. This stands in stark contrast to the design ideals Ken Parker founded his company upon: lighter instruments, more innovative designs and breaks from the accepted traditional elements of guitar design. It is unclear whether this change in management is what lead to Ken's distance from his former company, and why his current arch-top project seems very much a stand-alone department away from the rest of Parker.

In a January 2009 interview with Acoustic Guitar for 193rd issue, writer Baker Rorick calls Parker, "…a guitar iconoclast who has spent his life questioning conventions, but there's method to his madness and a sound reason behind every approach." Quite right. The interview focuses on Parker's new arch-top line, but seems to reinforce the luthier's belief that the modern guitar does not have to be as heavy as its forefathers to be effective. "I'm hoping my work will inspire some younger builders to lighten up their construction and see what these guitars are capable of." We shall see.

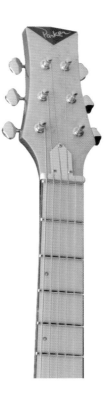

Parker

P8E

Parker's first acoustic guitar, the acoustic-electric P8E features a solid cedar top, rosewood binding, and solid flame maple back and flame maple sides. It has a mahogany neck with ebony microdot inlaid fingerboard and bridge. Electronics are a Fishman hum canceling pickup combined with their Acoustic Matrix undersaddle pickup. 1/4" and XLR outputs are provided. The guitar was first produced by Parker in 2005.

With their first release one can see the desire for preservation of Parker's original mission. The P8E bares a sans-traditional body style, not quite a dreadnought, not quite a jumbo-cutaway. It has a disarming beauty in its contour and unexpected lines. The truss rod is a light weight steel, and the overall heft required to keep the guitar around a player's shoulders much less strenuous. It is something of a compromise that the acoustic utilizes the Parker ethos friendly truss rod but accepts the traditional mahogany and maple for its body and fingerboard.

The move to a more corporate style of guitar production is no doubt due in no small part to the buyout of Parker Guitars. As we have seen historically, guitar companies only do well when they are taken over by larger guitar companies, not massive faceless corporations seeking a feather in their cap. Fender languishing under CBS for many years is just one example of what has been an industry trend since the 1960s. Hopefully, Parker has the wherewithal to withstand the big business model of guitar production long enough to retain its soul and continue producing the innovative instruments that the public has come to expect from it. The U.S. Music Corp., the company that owns Parker, also owns Washburn Guitars, Randall Amplifiers, Eden Amplifiers, SoundTech Professional Audio, Oscar Schmidt, Lyon Musical Instruments and Mojo Strings.

Right: Parker P8E front and back
Opposite page: Larry Coryell
playing a P8E guitar live on stage
at Ronnie Scotts United Kingdom

Parker on Display

Parker Guitars, known for their Ferrari-like design, unsurpassed playability, and lightweight construction have recently been placed on display at the Boston Museum of Fine Arts and the Boston Architectural Center. Their innovative design has contributed to the movement among luthiers that desire to create the acoustic and electric guitar as a living piece of art, as well as a musical instrument.

"Dangerous Curves," a unique guitar based exhibition put on by the Boston Museum of Fine Arts, placed a wonderful selection of instruments on display that highlighted guitars played by Jimi Hendrix, John Lennon, and others owned or played by music's most venerable players. Included in this amazing mixture of Americana, memorabilia and historical musical artifacts is a production model of the Parker Fly, the only post-1990 production guitar on display.

Seagull

S6 Cedar Original

In 1982 Robert Godin and a few friends produced the first Seagull guitars in the Village of LaPatrie, Quebec, where Godin Guitars is also headquartered. The concept for the Seagull guitar was to take the essential components of the best handcrafted guitars (such as solid tops and beautiful finishes) and build these features into guitars that could be priced within the reach of working musicians.

Winner of several awards, the S6 is perhaps the instrument that best represents the Seagull philosophy. The S6 offers entry level players the opportunity to experience the great feel and superb sound provided by a hand finished neck, select solid cedar top and a custom polished finish.

A Lesson in Guitar Craft

Seagull Acoustic Guitars could run a clinic on how an acoustic guitar works. "A guitar produces sound as a result of the vibration of its strings," writes the company, "What's not so obvious is the role that the guitar top plays in amplifying these vibrations. In fact, the vibration of the top is the most important factor in a guitar's sound. Solid top guitars offer richer sound and wider dynamic range (they play better at both soft and loud volume levels). The most interesting thing about a solid top guitar is that it will actually sound better over time...All Seagull guitars are made with select pressure tested solid tops. Each solid top is made from a single layer of spruce or cedar and is pressure tested to ensure its highest level of rigidity and stiffness along with maximum harmonic vibration."

How the Acoustic Guitar Ages

A solid top vibrates much more freely than a laminated (plywood) top. This results in richer tone, better dynamic range and better balance of tone. Not only does a solid top sound better initially, over time the vibrations from playing the guitar result in the top vibrating more and more freely. This phenomenon is called 'aging', which means that the more the guitar is played, the better the guitar will sound. It is important to remember that in order for a guitar to age, it must be played. A guitar left in its case for 5 years will get older, but it will not 'age'.

Materials are of the utmost importance when building any instrument. Seagull is finding a happy medium between the pressure to find the premium components without raising the price outside a tolerable range for the everyday musician. Their well developed knowledge has made them a slightly better version of an Epiphone to Godin's Gibson. They are an informative company, worth checking out for any guitar player starting out that is seeking a better understanding of how the instrument they love comes into being, or the more experienced player searching for a way to understand the finer techniques of luthiering in order to finally make that big splash purchase of a top-tier instrument.

Opposite page: Seagull S6
Cedar Original

Seagull

Artist Mosaic

The new compound curve top concept was originally developed for the Seagull Artist Series guitars and it is in these models that the new design has proven itself the most strongly. The Artist Series luthiers choose from the very best of a stockpile that includes over a hundred thousand, luthier-grade, solid cedar and spruce boards.

In fact, all of the tone woods for the Artist Series are hand selected to ensure that the very highest standards are met. The scalloped bracing is designed to such precise tolerances that it requires a CNC milling machine to carve the individual pieces to the exact specifications. The finished instruments speak with incredible clarity and character, all before they have been given a thorough play through. These guitars develop an even deeper character when 'played-in' and will no doubt become lifelong companions to those who choose them.

The solid cedar top arches slightly above the soundhole and slopes to level at the bridge to create a more stable top. This allows the use of ultra-thin scalloped bracing to deliver the most response and tone possible. The Artist Mosaic line is constructed with hand selected wood for the top, solid mahogany back, and mahogany/maple/mahogany sides for the ultimate in stability, warmth, and round, full timbre. Scintillating appointments include gold tuners, bound body and headstock, mother-of-pearl seagull inlay at the 12th fret and on the head, plus elaborate rosette.

What's Become of the Truss Rod?

Most guitars employ an adjustable metal rod inside the neck called a truss rod. The truss rod is typically used to straighten the neck when it becomes slightly bowed from string tension and changes in humidity. In the event of a neck becoming back-bowed the traditional fix is to loosen the truss rod and allow the string tension to pull the neck back to its ideal form. Unfortunately, this doesn't always work, which is why Seagull Guitars adapted a new double-action truss rod in their acoustic guitar necks. The new rod bends in both directions, which provides unprecedented control over the neck whether it is under-bowed or over-bowed.

The Seagull Body Styles

Seagull guitars come in three basic body sizes. The full sized body is used through most of the line including the cutaway models. Slightly smaller than a typical Dreadnought size guitar, the Seagull is narrower in the upper bout. This shape discourages unwanted "boominess" in the sound and is one of the factors that results in Seagulls being such excellent recording instruments.

The folk sized body shares its dimensions with those of a classical guitar and projects more midrange. The Folk models work beautifully for fingerstyle playing and solo guitar. The third Seagull body style is the compact body used in the Seagull Grand. The small body is tuned to produce a very clear fundamental, which makes it another excellent choice for fingerstyle playing. With such information at the company's disposal, it so no small wonder why Godin and Seagull both enjoy such positive player feedback and industry wide credibility.

Opposite page: Seagull Artist Mosaic Folk acoustic guitar and Seagull Artist Mosaic acoustic guitar

Nashville NV360's

Takamine takes its name from the mountain that the company's headquarters is built at the foot of in Sakashita, Japan. Takamine Guitars has over 40 years of history dedicated to innovation and improvement to the art and craft of guitar making. What first began as a small family business has evolved into one of the leading guitar manufacturers in the world, depended on by some of the best players and biggest names in the music industry. In order to understand Takamine's development and growing popularity, we will need to go back to 1960s Japan. That is when playing the guitar, and its greatest vehicle for the people, rock and roll, were becoming popular. As more people wanted to take up the instrument, the need for more guitars obviously increased. Takamine started manufacturing guitars during this time period, largely to meet these needs.

Demand only increased for quality guitars and Takamine met it head on, growing their business in the process. As a result of this, they hired Mr. Mass Hirade in 1968 to add skill and creative talent to their design team. They needed someone who could help develop and create guitars that would appeal to the changing musical tastes of the nation. One of his biggest contributions was the development of their (Japanese) Classical model, a guitar that achieved great popularity among those in Japan.

Takamine is known for two things: the quality of their instruments (Hirade played a big part in this) and their prices. They have an excellent budget line of guitars that has also achieved some popularity because even though they are inexpensive, they are known to have good quality.

The Nashville Series of Acoustic Guitars

The Takamine NV360's acoustic Guitar is handcrafted of all-solid woods by a special team at Takamine. Nashville models are as close to a luthier-built instrument as a buyer in the United States will find from an international guitar maker. The tops are solid, hand selected "bear claw" spruce, which creates a rare, naturally occurring pattern. Each soundboard is individually voiced to maximize its power and dynamic range. This particular Nashville is not towards the cheaper end of the Takamine line, though it does boast some of its best features.

The back and sides are solid, bookmatched Indian Rosewood, chosen for both its appearance and acoustic integrity. The ebony fingerboard is fitted with nickel silver frets, leveled and finished by hand for perfect playability and intonation. The soundhole and perimeter of the top are inlaid with hundreds of pieces of beautiful abalone shell. Nashville models are available in pure acoustic form, that is without the benefit (or detriment) of an active pickup system or preamp. As we can tell from the name of the series and as will be explained later, Takamine owes much of their success in the United States to the popularity boom of country music and those artists that flocked to Takamine for their affordable precision instruments.

Opposite page: Takamine acoustic guitar
Right: Takamine dragon detail

Takamine

Tradesman EF340'sBG

Currently Takamine has around twenty different guitar styles. Some of these are acoustic, some are electric, and some are acoustic/electric styles. These models include the Limited Edition 2006 Series, the Signature Series, the Takamini, the Naturals, the Supernaturals, and the Nashville. The guitars are designed to appeal to a range of tastes and style preferences.

The new Tradesman Series range of "purpose built" professional acoustic-electric guitars was conceived to provide the player with instruments that embody carefully considered elements that allow them to excel in specific musical environments. Built with luthier selected solid tone woods these instruments reflect the highest level of commitment to the art and craft of guitar making.

Guitars in the Series

The EF/TF340'sBG and EF/TF360'sBG "Flatpickers" are designs that pay homage to the past with vintage voicing, traditional looks and superb playability, while utilizing state of the art electronic packages to deliver every bit of the players' style and emotion to the audience. Pounding out a Bluegrass rhythm or tearing off a blazing "G" run, these guitars respond with absolute authority and have no fear of a heavy hand.

The TF430's "Singer Songwriter" is built to react accurately to the player's touch in a variety of musical styles. The tonality is warm and lush with a broad dynamic range. These guitars provide an excellent "sonic bed" to support a solo vocalist. The look is sweet vintage and the playing experience is pure inspiration.

Takamine Outside of Japan

In 1975 Hirade began exporting Takamine to other countries outside of Japan - the United States in particular. This era also marked the years when the guitar company would begin production of a different kind, and just in time. In 1978, Takamine began to introduce acoustic/electric guitars into the marketplace. Takamine acoustic/electric guitars grew to be a leading force in the flat back guitar market. The good word about Takamine was being spread, and musicians worldwide couldn't wait to get their hands on one. Their unique sound and look sparked the interest of acoustic guitar players almost instantly.

Innovations and Achievements

Takamine made great advancements with their palethetic pickup. This proprietary piece of equipment featured a clear, clean tone which complimented the acoustic guitar well and lent itself easily to electrification. With individually shielded six piezo-electric transducers, one for each string, the unit is hanged down and right beneath the bridge saddle. This unique design allows the pickup to be isolated from the vibration of the body, and enables each transducer to pick up the vibration of the string directly through the bridge saddle, which contributes to realizing an unmatched level of anti-feedback, even in a mega-volume environment. This in-house system of electronics is indicative of guitar companies as a whole, and it is interesting to see acoustic workshops that are "cut off" from the rest of the world market for several years innovating in similar ways as those companies that are not.

*Opposite page: Takamine
acoustic guitars*

Takamine

Supernaturals TAN77

Takamine's new SuperNatural series of instruments are available with the player's choice of solid cedar or solid spruce soundboards, and voiced for acoustic guitar players who appreciate brilliance and ambiance as much as depth and richness. Musicians will be able to feel the Takamine TAN77's acoustic power right through the solid rosewood back, braced and calibrated to enhance the broad range of the soundboard.

The Takamine TAN77 also features high ratio gold tuners for precise tuning capabilities, and abalone rosette with a tortoise pickguard. As an interesting innovation to this model, Takamine TAN77 comes with the new CoolTube (Takamine's latest proprietary electronic system) on-board tube preamp with bass and treble tone controls, semi-parametric midrange, a second-source input and blend control, and chromatic tuner. Electronics have always been the strength of the Asian market. Here is an area where Takamine has really been able to compete with the likes of American made Ovations who have been thought to have been the technological masters of the modern era in the United States.

Preamp Innovation

An exclusive Takamine innovation is the SoundChoice preamp system. All SoundChoice preamps are interchangeable and can be swapped in less than two minutes. This is also the hallmark of Japanese made automobiles, as they are highly customizable and easily replaced in terms of their parts. The preamp selections have been created as follows: Acoustic DSP: the first on-board digital preamp for acoustic guitar. This system includes parametric eq, a chromatic tuner and digital reverb for an almost unlimited range of sounds and effects. Accuracoustic: semi-parametric preamp with pinpoint control over frequency. It is especially useful for "acoustically-challenged" venues. CT-4B: a warm-sounding 3-Band graphic with an extremely stable and accurate chromatic tuner. This preamp is great for non-standard and open tunings. GRAPH-EX: A 3-band graphic equalizer that's calibrated to be easy to use and effective at shaping the character of your tone.

Takamine's Place in the U.S Market

The fact that Takamine acoustic guitars are so customizable has made them highly versatile and desirable among consumers. Ideally, only one guitar needs to be purchased, then the electronic systems go to work with the player analyzing the venue or particular place for a performance, deciding which system suits it the best and employing the proper kit from the Takamine tool belt. It makes perfect sense as something that Americans have come to expect from the Asian market, product that has literally thought of everything and does it well.

While the company has enjoyed success in the areas of electronics, and their sales were showing that the American market was ripe for their taking, Takamine still lacked that iconic artist to place as the face of their guitar company. Where Fender had Jimi Hendrix, Gibson had Robert Johnson, or Jimi Page, Takamine lacked that seminal artist to put a recognizable face on their instruments for the Western world to understand. At the ground level, a celebrity playing a guitar company's instrument is free advertising - both a gift and a curse - and Takamine needed it.

Opposite page: a closer look at the Takamine supernaturals Tan77 guitar

Takamine

Classics TH90

The Takamine TH90 Hirade Classic features a solid Spruce top with a solid Rosewood back and sides for a brilliant and rich classic tone. The braces are patterned and voiced for today's music. Hirade concert classics are crafted using Mass Hirade's original drawings. The Takamine TH90 Hirade Classic is equipped with the Takamine CoolTube Preamp. This on-board tube preamp features bass and treble tone controls, semi-parametric midrange, a second-source input and blend control, and chromatic tuner. These acoustic guitars, while semi-flamenco in appearance on the top and body style, are based from the drawings of Hirade.

Should the guitar player not care for the Cool Tube, there's little pressure to keep it, as Takamine Classics can be equipped with any one of four unique interchangeable SoundChoice preamps which provide maximum control over any performance application. The braces are patterned and voiced for today's music. The TH90 shows the versatility of the guitar company, creating nylon string guitars that have the same "plug-n-play" characteristics of the rest of Takamine's guitar roster.

Opposite page: Bruce Springsteen performing live onstage on the Devils and Dust tour, playing a Takamine acoustic guitar

Takamine

Above: Garth Brooks attends the 2009 Country Music Hall of Fame Medallion Ceremony

Garth Brooks GB7C

Takamine was waiting for their flagship artist, someone to carry the torch and be the face of their guitar lines for years to come; a homerun hitter, an icon. They found that artist in Garth Brooks. Brooks' signature guitar was worked on very closely by Garth as the design team brought the instrument from the drawing board to the stage. Garth's acoustic guitar has a solid cedar top, plus rosewood back and sides, providing tonal consistency and predictable sonic fullness from venue to venue.

The acceptance and access of the instrument to the plethora of electronic equipment that Takamine offers is paramount. Brooks often performed on stage without the use of cables or guitar chords, so he required an instrument that would be able to handle the appropriate equipment. If Takamine has an enumerated strength over another, it is their enduring and unyielding versatility.

Brooks has enjoyed one of the most successful careers in popular music history, breaking records for both sales and concert attendance throughout the 1990s. The RIAA has certified his recordings at a combined (128 platinum), denoting roughly 113 million U.S. shipments. Garth Brooks still continues to sell well - from the period of April 5th 2008 - September 26th 2008, he sold 277,000 albums in the U.S. taking his total album sales up to 68,051,000 - making him the bestselling artist in America since 1991, well over 11 million ahead of his nearest rival; The Beatles

Takamine and the Environment

C.F Martin & Co. is not the only guitar company with an eye towards protecting the environment. Japanese society already has some of the most advanced recycling equipment in the world, and breeds a culture that reduces their waste output and seeks to continually implement ways to better serve the land they have beneath them. Why shouldn't a guitar do the same?

Takamine's new Academy AC1 guitar is the right guitar for future guitar players and for our planet. This eco-friendly instrument is designed and constructed using sustainable timbers and water based ecologically responsible finishes and adhesives.

Crafted in Europe in the traditional classic guitar style, the nylon string AC1 features easy playability and excellent tone, which adds to the enjoyment of learning to play. Steel strings are often harder for a younger player to learn on, as their fingers are still growing and more sensitive to the pain that is associated with pressing into the strings, until the fingertips become used to the added pressure. The top is solid European Spruce and the body and neck are built using fine, European hardwoods that are plentiful and sustainable.

The Academy AC1 is the ideal instrument to present to school-based "guitar in the classroom" programs. Educators will appreciate the superb value of these instruments and students will enjoy the quality and durability of this fine guitar.

Taylor 810

Taylor Guitars has the rare distinction of being a guitar company which is still owned and operated by the person that founded it. Bob Taylor, a luthier that started in the business of guitar making at the age of 18, is still his own master many years later, at the helm of the company he helped create with Kurt Listug. The company is based in El Cajon, California.

Their beginnings were rough and lean. Taylor scratched hard to make a living in the early days of the company, working in a damp warehouse. How Taylor Guitars survived is a story of will and passion, elements integral to creating something that will carry on with a life of its own into the world. Taylor and Listug have made musical instrument history by becoming the first American luthiers in this century to take an acoustic guitar company from a one-off shop to a production-level manufacturer without relinquishing ownership or creative control.

The Original Flagship Model

The Taylor 810 is an acoustic that lives up to its pedigree with style, grace, and power. Known for its booming voice even before Taylor redesigned its bracing for added volume, the classic 810 is the dreadnought lover's dreadnought. It has plenty of presence and is now even more assertive. The India Rosewood used on this instrument seems like it was created for a guitar. Its clarity, balance, sustain, excellent bass response, wonderful coloration and figure are without equal. When paired with Sitka spruce, it is an unstoppable tonal combination. Other key features include a bound neck, an Indian Rosewood headstock overlay, 800 series fingerboard inlays, and a beautiful abalone rosette.

If You Can't Buy it, Build It

As a 17-year-old, he had seen a 12-string acoustic guitar in a local store window and lacking the funds to buy it, had decided to make his own. He built three guitars while still in high school, working on them at night in the back of a service station, in between filling gas tanks and wiping windshields. Eventually, Taylor took his finished instruments to Sam Radding at American Dream. Radding was convinced that he had a future in the trade.

During their first year at American Dream, Taylor and Listug made a few guitars, but mostly did repairs. When Radding decided to sell the business in 1974, the employees split into rival purchasing groups of two, each team jockeying for position while trying to figure out how to come up with the requisite capital. Finally, a triumvirate of Taylor, Listug, and Schemmer bought the American Dream. Euphoric with ambition, they renamed it the Westland Music Company.

"We thought that would sound impressive, and make people think we were bigger than we really were," Listug laughs. "But Bob was the real guitar-maker, and, besides, we had to have a logo that would fit on the headstock, so we soon named the guitars Taylor guitars." It is this independent spirit that has attracted musicians and guitar buyers alike since Taylor's inception, and what has ultimately kept them their own masters when every other small company has been swallowed whole.

Opposite page: Katy Perry performs on her Taylor 810 acoustic guitar
Left: a Taylor 810 guitar

Koa

The Taylor DN-K Dreadnought Acoustic Guitar has a Sitka spruce top and Hawaiian koa back & sides. This rare and exotic tonewood is prized for its stunning golden hues, bold grain figure, and sweet tone. Shimmering abalone trim around the top and soundhole complements the visual allure of the koa. Other features include ivoroid binding on the body, fingerboard, soundhole and peghead, an ebony headstock overlay, and gold-plated tuners.

The Taylor dreadnought is focused and assertive with plenty of presence and volume. The time-honored heritage of the dreadnought body style makes it the choice of the traditional player. Taylor produces several variants of the koa in order to incorporate body styles and accommodate individual player need.

Selling that First Guitar

"Those first guitars had some structural problems, and sometimes the backs would ripple," Listug recalls. "We knew they couldn't compete, aesthetically, with the best guitars on the market, so we just kept working at it until we had a marketable-looking guitar."

After selling a few prototypes at the workshop, the partners decided to take their wares directly to dealers. In 1976, Listug loaded some guitars into Bob Taylor's van and headed for the music stores in Los Angeles. "They liked them, and I actually came home with checks in my hand," Listug says. The genuine candor of Listug's recollections shows the character of Taylor Guitars as a whole. They were a couple of kids with a dream that took a chance on doing what they loved. While this doesn't always work out, it is a plan that has come to fruition enough times that people believe that hard work pays off.

One of the first dealers to buy a Taylor guitar was the venerable McCabe's, in Santa Monica. John Zehnder, who today is the store's chief repairman, director of its music school, and banjo and mandolin instructor, remembers those first Taylors. "In 1976, Taylors provided an affordable and viable alternative to Martins, which were the standard," Zehnder said in a phone interview. "The Taylors' low-profile necks, and the fact that they offered several choices as to neck widths, were a real advantage. Plus, they sounded good, and, because of the way they were made [with bolt-on necks], we were able to make repairs instantly, which was greatly appreciated by our customers. In many ways, Taylor guitars were a real breath of fresh air."

That plug-and-play aspect of guitar making is something that foreign companies, like Takamine in Japan, are all too familiar with. For Taylor, the ease in repair work after market was created in the shop to facilitate quick building and low stress for what at the time was a very small staff. Still, there was no watershed success for Taylor as the larger acoustic guitar companies still held sway over a majority of the market. Taylor would be checking their receipts and saving pennies well into the 1980s.

Left: Taylor Baby acoustic guitar
Opposite page: a closer look at the
Taylor KOA 24 CE acoustic guitar

The GS

Introduced in 2006, the GS is an original design from top to bottom, and represents the first new Taylor shape in over a decade. It was an immediate hit with acoustic guitar players. You can expect acoustic power with every note, with deep, piano-like bass, rich mids and clear, balanced highs-and plenty of volume. It's a whole new flavor of Taylor tone.

The GS Series is comprised of four different models. These guitars will not adopt the numbering conventions of the other Taylor shapes with a model in the 300 series, the 400 series, the 500 series, etc. Additionally, each model is essentially the same except for the discerning difference of being crafted with a unique combination of high-quality traditional tonewoods.

The lineup consists of the GS rosewood/spruce, the GS maple/spruce, GS mahogany/cedar, and the GS rosewood/cedar. Each has a 25.5" scale, mahogany neck, and ebony fingerboard. The fingerboard has abalone microdot fret markers and 20 medium-jumbo frets. The bridge is made with ebony as well, and the headstock faceplate overlay is rosewood. All the binding (body, neck, headstock) is ivoroid and the soundhole rosette is abalone. Each piece is applied with the fit, finish and reparability that is Taylor's industry reputation. A high gloss finish completes the series ambiance. The look is understated if almost classic, thereby putting the focus where it belongs: on the sound and playability.

Ready to Weather Any Storm

"Those early years were nothing but day after day of bad news," says the company's co-founder Bob Taylor. "But we're better off for it. It's a really great market for acoustic guitars right now, and I think there are some guitar makers doing well because it's a great market. They're getting a lot of money for their product, but they're wasteful in their thinking and in their handling of money and materials. So, if the market goes south again, and prices tighten up, and we're all fighting over the same sales, those people might not be prepared for it. We know what those conditions are like - what that's all about - so, we'd be in better position to weather the storm. I'd hate like heck to have to go through all that bad stuff again. But, right now, I'm glad we did. We're a better, more resilient company because of it."

That market does appear to be changing, due mostly the shrink of the global economy radiating outward from a United States financial crisis. Guitar companies are forced to work harder than ever to resist the urge to sell to a larger corporation to ease their financial burdens. Taylor's wisdom may be put to the test sooner than he realizes, and this time the rent may not be just $160.

This page: Taylor Swift performs on stage during the Sound Relief concert at Sydney Cricket Ground Opposite page: the Taylor GS acoustic guitar

Washburn

Vintage WSJ 124K

In celebration of 125 years of fine stringed instruments, Washburn introduces three masterful reproductions of guitars built in the late 1800s. These guitars have been skillfully "antiqued" to appear as if they have suffered over 100 years of wear. These lovingly recreated versions of popular guitars have all the benefits of modern technology with all the romance and passion of The Golden Era of guitar craftsmanship.

These are the full circle style instruments, those crafted that make it a point to use the production methods of the here and now while employing the style or motif of the past. Washburn is a company that has built a quiet empire from these weather-beaten acoustics, only to branch out into the electric guitar world as well.

A Long, Long Time Ago...

The Washburn guitar company started making guitars in 1883 in Chicago under the watchful eye of George Washburn Lyon. The factory would later be involved and located near a musical movement in Chicago in the 1920s. The Delta Blues arrived in Chicago by way of traveling musicians playing gigs in a different venue each night, creating a tone and voice that was unheard of at that time. This type of approach to the acoustic guitar would change the way music was played, and would also provide the foundations for what would become rock and roll. Washburn saw an opportunity with the blues, and moved to design guitars these players would want.

As it so happened, Washburn guitars ended up being the benefactors of geography. Maxwell Street, a hotbed of venues and blues clubs in the 1920s, sat only moments from where Washburn's first factory operated from. It was an easy task getting out to watch these blues players ply their craft, see how they worked their instruments, and what materials and body styles would suit them best. It was all downhill after that. The history of Washburn Guitars is the history of a wide range of musicians - from blues players who shaped rock 'n' roll to multi-platinum recording artists to emerging guitar virtuosos. It is a history that can be heard and experienced every time you turn on the radio or listen to a live performance. It is a history built by skilled craftsmen and musicians who share one common love: a passion for the guitar.

Washburn makes electric guitars, acoustic guitars, electric basses, acoustic basses, banjos, mandolins, travel guitars, and amplifiers. The company also makes accessories including guitar cases, clothing, and other parts like tuners, pickups, and straps. Washburn is mostly known for its electric guitars and acoustic guitars. The company makes eight different styles or "Series" of both electric and acoustic guitars. The Vintage series is a retelling of that exciting time in the history of Washburn when all was bustling and bristling with creation. Newly formed companies are at a disadvantage with this particular design, only having the ability to craft "vintage style" instruments of bygone eras that they did not participate within. Washburn is able to use his participation as a selling point. The company is currently owned by the U.S. Music Corporation.

*Above: From left to right: AB-40
Vintage, AB40SHK Black Cherry
Burst, AB40SHK Natural
Oppopsite page: Washburn
acousic guitar*

Washburn

Vintage R 314K

To continue the celebration of their 125th anniversary, Washburn released this vintage version of an early 1900s Parlor style acoustic. This acoustic guitar is slightly smaller than traditional instruments and significantly smaller than the dreadnought but serves its purpose of performance in a small, intimate space. The reviews for this particular model have not been kind. "I've owned this guitar almost a year, a tuner went bad," writes one Vintage owner, "The bridge started to rise up due to no glue between the rear of the bridge and the finished top - revealing laminated spruce, although it is described as 'aged look spruce top', not mentioning the lamination." Consumer feedback goes a long way to a company's success. It is possible that larger factories produce a significantly larger quantity of errors in instruments, which we have seen with other companies that are using the resources of multi-national organizations.

The Good Press

Washburn does have award winning instruments however, and they are endorsed by both professional as well as amateur musicians who rely on the company's dedication to high standards of quality in order to meet their creative needs. Washburn's innovative designs include features such as the Buzz Feiten Tuning System, which allows for a perfectly tuned guitar, and the Stephens Extended Cutaway, a modification of the standard bolt neck construction that allows for easy access to the upper register of the guitar fret board. Washburn also boasts an extensive list of guitarists who love their instruments. These include Aaron Fink of Breaking Benjamin, Wes Scantlin of Puddle of Mudd, Sonny Mayo of Sevendust, Ryan Pierce of Neal McCoy, Paul Stanley of KISS, Paul Crook of Meatloaf, and Rick Savage of Def Leppard.

All of these wonderful creations are coming from Washburn's custom shop, which is still based in the United States. There has been little mention of Washburn's overseas construction methods since its purchase by the U.S. Music Corp., though the company does maintain home offices in Illinois - Washburn Guitars calls this home as well.

Acoustic Guitars By The Way Side

The majority of companies that are still producing guitars in the United States began by producing acoustic guitars of some variant. Over time some of those companies have chosen to focus on the electric guitar as the future of where music is going, as opposed to the acoustic, which has been relegated to smaller runs and fewer series standouts. Washburn is a company that has thrown its hat in the ring when it comes to the electric, and done so with great success.

Guitar manufacturers must be careful to not forget where they come from. The acoustic guitar is the blueprint for the wild innovations of the electrified instruments of today and will always provide that base level design element. Companies that maintain a healthy acoustic guitar division, like Gibson, Fender and Godin have historically garnered a larger share of the market and public consciousness.

Opposite page: a closer look at the Washburn Vintage R 314K acoustic guitar

Washburn

Jumbo Series J 27CE

The Java Ebony on the J27CE is the foundation for the beautiful looks and tone that make this a truly impressive guitar. The BBand system will give you the closest tone to an acoustic amplified by a microphone so a player can easily get on stage. The jumbo maple body with solid spruce top sounds awesome unplugged as well. The Cumberland Series guitars have been a staple in the Washburn line for over 15 years and are at home on stage and in the studio.

Night and Day for the Design Team

As beautiful and quality a guitar as the ones created in the Jumbo series by Washburn are, it's difficult to imagine the shop could churn out misfires like the Vintage Parlor. That said, the Jumbo is the more modern style and one that has been embraced by the modern guitar player as well.
The acoustic guitar is a merciless mistress when it comes to detail. Everything on the guitar must be well cared for, or the entire instrument will sound like cardboard on a rainy day. We have seen time and again that adhesives used poorly ruin the potential for a quality instrument which is often a place where a larger, numbers-oriented shop will skimp first - thinner wood materials usually follow. This often results in the damage we have seen here in this history: cracks in the neck of the guitar, finishes not adhered properly to the wood, resulting in peeling and a kind of bubbling of the material. Of all the instruments that are at the disposal of the modern guitar player, the acoustic is the one that requires the most fundamental level of skill to play and to create. Chords ring loudly on them; missed strings plunk like chicken wire; woods of less than ideal quality crack and bow under the tension they create to perform well. There are entire rosters of bands that would never be able to do MTV's very popular series of Unplugged shows simply because they lack the technical skill necessary to transmit a

song played well on an electric guitar, to the more demanding acoustic. This is why Eric Clapton is one the greatest guitar players to have ever lived, because of his technical skill, slow-hand virtuosity, and the ability to translate a tune from the scream of an electric to the sultry resonance of the acoustic guitar.

Some companies are in danger of overlooking the acoustic as time marches forward, ignoring the very foundations that created the movements for the current instruments they now design. The future of the instrument may rest with something more electric, and it would be hard to argue that the star power involved in the chugging lines and soaring solos of by an electric, but for the acoustic guitar, as evidenced by the guitars and companies producing them, has much more room for innovation, still.

Opposite page: a closer look at the Washburn J27CEK guitar
Right: Washburn acoustic electirc guitar with Stephen Jensen graphics

Yamaha

Handcrafted series CJ32

Corporate giant Yamaha has been an innovator and designer of everything from keyboards, to guitars, to motorcycles. There is seemingly nothing on the map that they cannot grasp hold of and bend to their will. As a company, they have been building musical instruments since the late 1800s (more accurately in 1887, the first instrument being an organ). In 1942, they debuted their first acoustic guitar - by then, the company had been in business for almost fifty years, so they were already known for their instruments and musical products. Yamaha's product line has since expanded. At one point, they even had an archery products business.

The Handcrafted Series

For country music performers, nothing makes a finer playing companion than Yamaha's CJ32 Country Jumbo - an instrument that possesses the distinct look of a high class instrument. The combination of a solid spruce top and solid flamed maple back and sides produces a gutsy, well balanced tone with crisp, clearly defined highs and solid, resonant lows; a sound that cuts through like very few other acoustic guitar designs. But is it actually handmade? Yamaha is not divulging anything.

The guitar certainly looks the part; abalone adorns the soundhole rosette and body binding, the bound ebony fingerboard carries beautiful split-triangle pearl position markers, while the sculpted ebony bridge conjures up the showmanship of the Wild West. Resplendent in its richly hued sunburst finish, the CJ32 is truly a visual and aural treat. Yamaha is riding an interesting line, attempting to seem like the small luthier's workshop amidst the corporation that surrounds its musical arm. They do present a unified front however, as they "lack" the iconic luthier or crafter of instruments that birthed them and have Yamaha a signature look or style. In a way, this is a massive strength. Yamaha does not know what a Yamaha guitar looks like, and neither do we, which means it could come from any discipline in music. Should Yamaha design a flamenco guitar for the hottest clubs in Spain, consumers would buy it without questioning the company's "credibility" to design such an instrument. It is Yamaha, they design custom motorcycles and bows & arrows, what makes anyone think that they cannot create (at the very least) a comparable nylon string acoustic.

As a company, Yamaha has earned the right to try certain things, experiment, and exist outside the boundary of trend and market fluctuations. Whereas a smaller workshop like Godin, or Taylor may have to batten down the hatches in order to weather the current economic storm, Yamaha will be able to continue offering instruments at their current prices, perhaps creating a few cheaper ones to keep their product face out there. As we will see later, Yamaha is continuing that same spirit of innovation and corporate assurance right under the noses of the rest of the industry. A guitar player could buy three Yamaha acoustic guitars for the half the price of a Martin D-28.

Opposite page: Handcrafted Yamaha guitars

*Left: Yamaha Silent Series
SLG 100N guitar
Opposite page: Yamaha Silent
Series SLG 100N guitar*

Silent Series SLG100N

The Silent Guitar allows the player to practice with headphones, yet still enjoy the realistic sound of an acoustic instrument. The nylon-stringed SLGS100N features a lightweight composite body, mahogany neck, rosewood fingerboard, and breaks down quickly to fit into included gig bag for easy transport. Electronics include piezo in-bridge pickups and an internal DSP which reproduces the natural sounding reverb of a user selected acoustic space. This guitar also has mini-stereo inputs for plugging in a CD player for play along. Interfaces with the AG Stomp.

A Design Like No Other

The Yamaha Silent Guitar was originally designed as an ideal practice and travel instrument. But the nylon string SLG100N quickly became popular with touring guitarists enamored with its practical, feedback free live applications and modern jet age appearance. Elegant design and sonic solutions are Yamaha traditions. Yamaha continues to innovate with the Silent Series.

The sound it produces acoustically is minimal, but when a musician slips on a pair of headphones, the player enters a virtual world where full, rich classic guitar tone is enveloped in luxurious reverb; a world full of space and beauty. For beginners or experienced players alike, the Silent Guitar will provide you with pleasure through great playability and tone.

The SLG100N has custom-designed pickup systems by L.R. Baggs, and the B-Band faithfully reproduce every nuance, providing full, rich tone for stage and studio work. This Yamaha Silent guitar also features great sounding built in Yamaha digital reverbs. Backstage, on the tour bus, or at home, the SLG100 easily fulfills the role of a woodshed axe, thanks to its comfortable, lightweight composite frame and included earbud-style headphones. With the AUX IN jack, musicians can connect a CD player for private jamming.

When finished, the SLG100N quickly dismantles and stores in the included compact gig bag for easy storage and travel. The Yamaha Silent guitar works with batteries or the included power supply. The Yamaha SLG100N is a silent guitar for anyone who needs to keep quiet in a dorm, apartment, condo or hotel room. It features a lightweight body with a Mahogany neck and Rosewood fingerboard that breaks down quickly for easy transportation.

Significance of Silence

The play with design, in terms of an acoustic guitar's body, shows other companies out there that the acoustic guitar still, after over 4,000 years since the first men strung sinew over wood, has room for further innovation and experimentation. Conventions must be tested, manipulated and tweaked in order to find - not so much the perfect form - but to allow addition to the vast variety that already exists in the musical world.

It comes from a surprising source. Yamaha, while one of the largest companies examined here in this history, is not thought of widely as an "elite" creator of acoustic guitars the world over. Perhaps it is then fair to say that "elite" is not such an appropriate term after all. To be in that class where everything created is thought to be gold is a lot of pressure to live up to. Everyone knows what to expect from a Martin guitar, what a Gibson Jumbo might look like, but Yamaha still manages to take creative license in the midst of all that corporate cash.

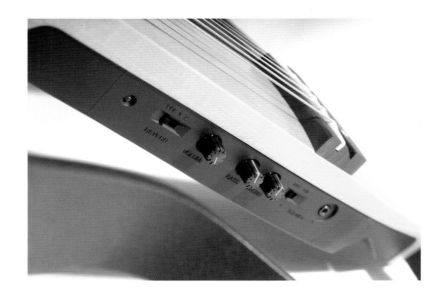

Zemaitis

GZAT100-Heart

Guitars that look beautiful and play just as well is what inspired the creation of Zemaitis Guitars, and the Heart model acoustic. Its Indian rosewood body plays up a simple elegance with its 3-piece mahogany neck. Its "heart" shape comes from its Jumbo body style and intricate rosette around the sound hole.

Art Guitars and Starting Out

Antanus Casimere Zemaitis, or Tony, was born in London, England in 1935. As a child he was constantly designing and building – everything from model flying airplanes to handmade bicycles. His creative talents first led him to cabinetry, where he learned invaluable skills in working with wood, design and decoration.

In the 1950s, as a young guitar player, Tony was unsatisfied with the available guitars of the times. So taking cues from a friend's classical guitar, he decided to build his own - the first Zemaitis guitar. From then on, it was a lifelong quest to hone his craft and experiment with new designs and materials in order to improve every guitar he made – a characteristic that would follow him throughout his life. He attracted the initial interest of the London blues and folk scene, which is where he played his instruments and hung out with other musicians of that sphere. Slowly those around him began to ask questions and inquire who made his guitars. Tony's reputation grew from there.

By the 1980s, his reputation for workmanship, styling, playability and tonal quality had made Tony Zemaitis a living legend. While highly coveted by collectors, Tony did not restrict his customers to just the rich and famous, and always remained true to his ideals. Though he worked primarily by himself, producing just a handful of guitars every year, Tony was just as happy to work with enthusiastic amateur guitarists and even sold 'student' grade models to those with lower budgets.

Opposite page: a closer look at the Zemaitis GZAT 100-Heart acoustic guitar

No matter what grade of guitar he constructed, he always produced a great playing and sounding guitar. He always used quality materials and traditional luthier techniques, such as 3-piece necks and bodies for strength and stability and only ever use glued-neck construction to ensure the best possible sound.

It was the combination of quality, craftsmanship, innovation and determination that won this British guitar maker fans from all over the world. After forty years of handcrafting fine guitars and having virtually created the 'boutique guitar', Tony retired in 2000. He passed away on August 17, 2002. Those hand-crafted instruments that Zemaitis produced are his link with the mortal world, a tangible sense of immortality. Musical notes are ageless; they do not fade over time or ring less significantly than they did the last time they were struck. For the luthier, the truest test of their instruments is whether the instruments they have so carefully built by hand over many hours are still being played long after they are gone. For Tony Zemaitis, that is an easy test to pass.

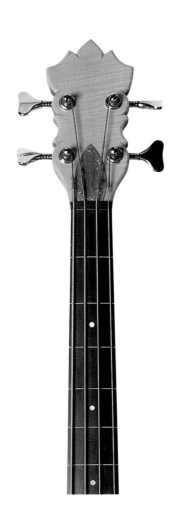

GZA200-SUN

What is so eye catching about these acoustic guitars is the slight variation on shape and the aesthetic appeal this can cause. The guitar looks like it wants to be picked up, like the sound is bright, clear, and resonant. All the hardware and tone woods that are used in the heart design acoustic are used with the sun acoustic, only the intricate inlays are different. In truth, a guitar player might not notice the difference between the two if forced to pick both up blindfolded. The wood inlay is complex to go along with abalone used for the rosette.

Carrying on Without Zemaitis

A significant portion of carrying on the Zemaitis tradition can be attributed to the services of Danny O'Brien, the master engraver who worked with Tony Zemaitis for many years. Danny's tremendous skills and artistry have helped the guitar company that Zemaitis left behind ensure the continued authenticity and craftsmanship of his creations and preserve the integrity of his original designs.

Danny O'Brien designs the unique and beautiful engravings for Zemaitis Metal Front guitars and all the other Zemaitis Guitar metal components, including the badge, truss rod cover, pickup mount rings, tailpiece, jackplate, and the rear plate. The work is then completed by hand by Zemaitis guitars' team of shotgun engravers, schooled in the same techniques as Danny.

Danny's new designs are helping carry out the history started by Tony Zemaitis. The company appears excited for the next chapter of the company just recently left behind by their creator. They have already begun the greater task of putting a Zemaitis guitar in the hands of a famous musician with their custom series for Ronnie Wood (Rolling Stones), Joe Walsh, Billy Sheehan, Sully Erna (Godsmack), Chris Robinson (The Black Crowes), among many others. The company also just ran across an old film of George Harrison playing a Zemaitis acoustic on the song, "Faster." For Zemaitis, it's only a matter of time before greater notice is taken of them.

At the Close

Tony Zemaitis, like Bob Taylor, C.F Martin, Leo Fender, and Fred Gretsch, was a man with a simple desire. To create a guitar that sounded the way he wanted it to sound. For so many guitar players of all genres, tone is the most important issue, not the gloss or the bells and whistles or the pearl inlays. What did the guitar sound like? Since the stringed instrument's beginnings, that is what has driven him. If the first man to string cat gut over a chambered soundhole didn't like what he heard we may have had to wait another thousand years before the memory of that sour note had faded properly. The history of the acoustic guitar is a continuing one, one that searches for the next available means to give the newest guitar player what they want, the tone they desire, the playability they need. The greatest innovators here are not the luthiers, or the guitar companies with their factories and workshops and many-roomed warehouses. It is the player - the musician - that will show the way to the next path.

Opposite page: Ronnie Lane playing his Zemaitis acoustic guitar

GZAT100-T

The Zemaitis GZAT 100-T is of a line that is the smallest the guitar company currently sells, and is geared towards offering that signature Zemaitis tone at an affordable price for the acoustic guitar player. Modeled very closely after the Sun and Hart acoustic models, the 100's "tiny" body is a mere 12.9h/328mm with a scale of 23"1/2 inches and only 19 frets, one less than the modernly accepted standard for acoustics and several less than modern electrics.

The top of the guitar is made from solid spruce with its back and sides being built from rosewood. The use of the latter wood may be deemed more economical due to the guitar's small stature. Its neck is one piece and built from mahogany, with the joint occurring at the 14th fret. The sound hole and bridge are artfully crafted to give the appearance that the GZAT is smiling up at the guitar player, as if looking out on those gathered around and agreeing with the company. The headstock still sports the traditional and familiar "Z" emblazoned in metal.

Greco Guitars

Zemaitis also offers the GZ Series in an electric guitar format and is manufactured with a license from Greco, Japan's predominant quality guitar builders. With more than 40 years of experience in designing, building, and wholesaling high quality guitars, the small team at Greco is proud to be making these prestigious instruments. Greco is a brand of electric guitars created by Kanda Shokai in Japan. Much of that company's notoriety comes from being a part of Fender's Japanese wing of production and development but has had a long history (over sixty years) of experience in crafting fine instruments. They garnered a quick reputation (much like other Japanese guitar makers) for crafting Gibson and Fender-like instruments in the '70s and '80s. Perhaps this led Fender to finally buy the company out, maybe saying, "If we can't stop them, we'll put them to good use."

Zemaitis has managed to remain their own masters in a world where companies and small guitar workshops are being bought up by larger organizations. Some, like Fender and Gibson, are well intentioned in their pursuits and the products of these guitar makers have flourished under them. As there exists still that corporate giant that seeks only another feather in its cap, for this reason, Zemaitis fights hard to retain the reins of its future, and ensure that the spirit of the man who created it lives on.

Opposite page: Ronnie Lane
playing Zemaitis acoustic guitar

Guitar Timeline

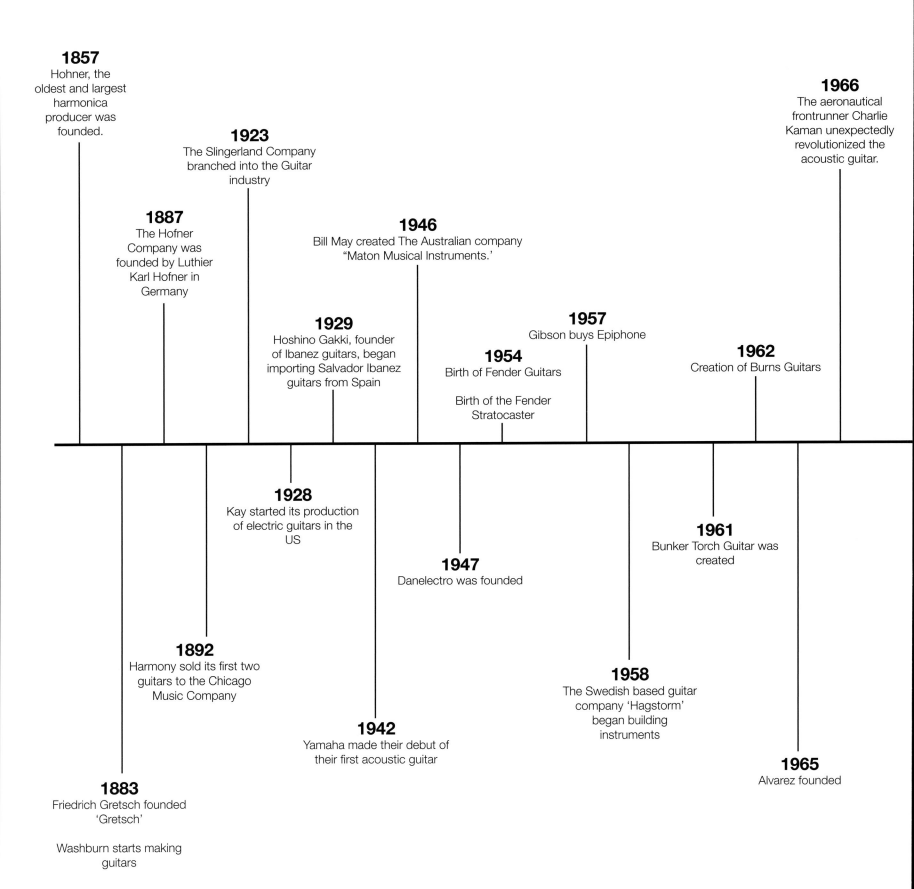

1857
Hohner, the oldest and largest harmonica producer was founded.

1966
The aeronautical frontrunner Charlie Kaman unexpectedly revolutionized the acoustic guitar.

1923
The Slingerland Company branched into the Guitar industry

1887
The Hofner Company was founded by Luthier Karl Hofner in Germany

1946
Bill May created The Australian company "Maton Musical Instruments.'

1929
Hoshino Gakki, founder of Ibanez guitars, began importing Salvador Ibanez guitars from Spain

1957
Gibson buys Epiphone

1954
Birth of Fender Guitars

Birth of the Fender Stratocaster

1962
Creation of Burns Guitars

1928
Kay started its production of electric guitars in the US

1961
Bunker Torch Guitar was created

1947
Danelectro was founded

1892
Harmony sold its first two guitars to the Chicago Music Company

1958
The Swedish based guitar company 'Hagstorm' began building instruments

1942
Yamaha made their debut of their first acoustic guitar

1965
Alvarez founded

1883
Friedrich Gretsch founded 'Gretsch'

Washburn starts making guitars

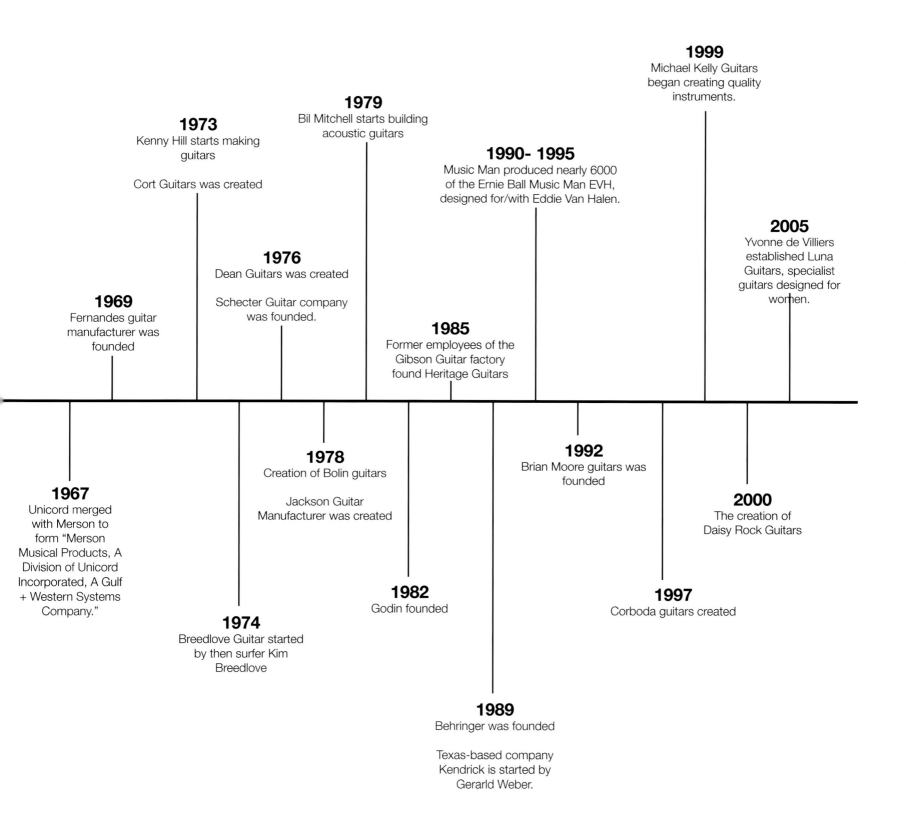

1999
Michael Kelly Guitars
began creating quality
instruments.

1979
Bil Mitchell starts building
acoustic guitars

1973
Kenny Hill starts making
guitars

Cort Guitars was created

1990- 1995
Music Man produced nearly 6000
of the Ernie Ball Music Man EVH,
designed for/with Eddie Van Halen.

2005
Yvonne de Villiers
established Luna
Guitars, specialist
guitars designed for
women.

1976
Dean Guitars was created

Schecter Guitar company
was founded.

1969
Fernandes guitar
manufacturer was
founded

1985
Former employees of the
Gibson Guitar factory
found Heritage Guitars

1978
Creation of Bolin guitars

Jackson Guitar
Manufacturer was created

1992
Brian Moore guitars was
founded

1967
Unicord merged
with Merson to
form "Merson
Musical Products, A
Division of Unicord
Incorporated, A Gulf
+ Western Systems
Company."

2000
The creation of
Daisy Rock Guitars

1982
Godin founded

1997
Corboda guitars created

1974
Breedlove Guitar started
by then surfer Kim
Breedlove

1989
Behringer was founded

Texas-based company
Kendrick is started by
Gerarld Weber.

Acknowledgements

The publishers would like the thank the following picture libraries for their kind permission to use their pictures and illustrations:

Istock photolibrary: 10, 14, 15, 19, 29, 31, 32, 44, 47, 50, 51, 53, 56, 77, 79, 80, 82, 88, 91, 100, 104, 107, 108, 112, 114, 115, 141, 147

Balafon Image Bank, managed by Jawbone Press: 12, 13, 39, 60, 61, 63, 74, 133, 134, 135, 136, 137, 139, 143, 144, 146, 148, 149, 161, 167, 201

Getty Images: 17, 18, 32, 37, 54, 59, 64, 69, 71, 75, 76, 92, 95, 96, 99, 102, 110, 130, 131, 132, 140, 152, 155, 157, 159, 162, 164, 165, 166, 172, 184, 186, 189, 192, 207, 208

Alvarez: 8, 9, 11

Corboda: 20, 21, 22, 23

Daisy Rock Girl Guitars: 24, 25, 26, 27

Dean Guitars: 28

Epiphone: 35, 36, 38, 39, 40, 41, 42, 43

Fender: 45, 46, 47, 48, 49, 52, 57, 58

Gibson: 66, 68, 70, 72, 73,

Godin: 85, 86, 87

Hohner: 109

Ibanez: 118, 119

Luna Guitars: 120, 121, 123, 124, 125, 126, 127

Mitchell Guitars: 150, 151, 153

Parker: 168, 169, 170, 171, 173

Seagull: 175, 177

Takamine: 178, 179, 181, 183, 185

Taylor: 188, 190, 191, 193

Washburn: 194, 195, 196, 197, 198. 199

Yamaha: 6, 7

Zemaitis: 204, 205

Every effort has been made to contact the copyright holders for images reproduced in this book. Any omissions are entirely unintentional, and the details should be addressed to Quantum Publishing.

Glossary

A

Abalone – an ornate shell material commonly used on instrument inlays. Abalone inlays come in a rainbow of colors and can appear to change color when viewed from different angles. Sometimes also called "mother of pearl".

Action - the string height above the tops of the frets.

Active - when pickups are said to be active they incorporate a pre-amp which requires additional power. The result is a boost and/or wider range for the pickup.

Archtop - a guitar which has been carved or pressed. The bridge and tailpiece are movable. Generally used by Jazz musicians.

Bakelite - early form of plastic used in some guitars from the 30s to the 50s.

Bigsby - a simple non-recessed vibrato developed by Paul Bigsby.

B

Binding - a protective and decorative strip made of wood or plastic that is placed along the outer most edges of the top, back, neck, fingerboard and some times headstock. This is a cap used to seal and protect joints. Sometimes incorrectly referred to as purfling, purfling actually refers to inlays along side of the binding and not the actual binding itself.

Block Markers - square, rectangular or shark tooth inlays marking fingerboard position.

Body - the main portion of the guitar which the controls, bridge and pickups are mounted.

Bolt On - an instrument that has its neck attached by bolts rather than being glued in place.

Bookmatched - most acoustic and many archtop guitars have tops and backs that are 2 pieces of wood glued together to form one large panel. Bookmatched refers to the wood coming from the same tree and actually being one piece of wood that has been but into consecutive slices so the grain in the panels creates mirror image patterns.

Brace - wooden struts glued to the insides of hollowbody guitars providing strength and affecting tone quality. An X-brace is a popular brace pattern used in hollowbody guitars. Other bracing patterns include the ladder brace, fan bracing and scalloped braces.

Bridge - bridges come in a variety of shapes and sizes. On a solid body electric guitar they generally fixed and hold the saddle that makes contact with the strings. On archtop guitars the bridge is usually held in place only by the tension of the strings and can be easily moved, also called a "floating bridge".

Bridge Pins – pins that anchor the strings on to the bridge

C

CAP - a common electrical component that stores up an electrical charge generally used on the tone potentiometer on electric guitars.

Celluloid - plastic material used on guitar pickguards, tuners and binding. This material is not very durable and deteriorates over time therefore many vintage guitars have issues with celluloid parts.

Center Block - the solid wood block running through the body of a semi-acoustic guitar body.

Checking - cracking found in lacquer finished guitars. Vintage guitars often have checking in their lacquer finishes caused by the guitar's wood expanding and contracting with changes in temperature and humidity.

Cutaway – a guitar which has been cut away to allow easy access to the frets while reaching over the body. A double cut guitar away has both sides cut away. Usually referred to as "singlecut" and "doublecut" guitars.

D

Dog Ear - a P-90 style pickup with mounting ears.

Dot Neck – a guitar with simple dot inlays in the neck position markers.

E

Electro Acoustic - an acoustic guitar with a built in pickup, often a piezo electric pickup.

End block - acoustic guitars normally have an end block and a neck block at opposite ends of the body. The end block is usually glued to the top, back, and sides at the bottom end of the guitar. Often strap buttons are are anchored into this block as it provides the strength necessary to support a strap.

F

F-hole - an "f" shaped sound hole on some hollowbody and semi-acoustic guitars.

Fingerboard (also called a fretboard) - the surface of the neck that contains the frets. Note there are also some guitars that are "fretless" but the fingerboard is still used without frets. The fingerboard is generally a separate piece of wood glued to the neck. It's often made of a hard durable wood as the frets must be securely anchored into the fretboard. Vintage guitars often used Brazilian Rosewood and Ebony for fingerboard material.

Finish - the protective coating covering the guitar, often paint or lacquer.

Fixed Bridge - non-vibrato bridges.

Flame - sometimes also called Flame Top. Generally refers to Maple with dramatic grain resembling flames.

Flat Top - an acoustic guitar with a flat (non-arched) top. Many Martin and Gibson guitars are considered flat top acoustic guitars.

Fret - metal wire inlayed at intervals along the fingerboard. The guitar player presses down on the string forcing the string to touch the fret changing the sting length and producing different notes. There are a variety of fret wire profiles used for frets.

H

Hang Tag - small tags and cards hung on guitars in show rooms. A hang tag for a vintage guitar is generally very difficult to find.

Hard Tail - an electric guitar without a vibrato bridge, often used to describe Fender guitars.

Headstock - the part of the guitar where the strings attach to the tuners.

Heel - portion of neck where the neck curves or is reduced to join the body.

Hollow Body - an electric guitar body style with a thin body similar to an acoustic guitar.

Humbucker - a noise canceling twin coil pickup.

I

Inlay – the decorative material that is cut and embedded into the body, neck or headstock of a guitar.

Intonation - the guitars ability to play in tune at various positions along the neck. Often adjusted by adjusting the bridge saddle.

J

Jackplate - mounting plate for output jack.

L

Laminated - the backs, sides and even tops of some instruments can be made from several pieces of wood which have been laminated to form one piece, usually at the expense of sound quality.

Locking Nut - bolts that lock the strings in place at the nut.

Luthier - a guitar maker and guitar repair expert.

Glossary

M

Machine Heads - also knows as tuners or tuning machines. Allows string tension to be changed changing the pitch of the strings.

N

Neck Block - the neck block is found inside of the body at the base of the neck. The Neck block provides a strong point to mount the neck to the body.

Neck Plate - a metal plate used in the Fender style bolt on designs, it is screwed to the neck and the body fastening the neck to the guitar body.

Neck Pickup - the pickup closest to the neck.

Neck Reset - a neck reset is performed restore the correct angle between the fingerboard bridge which provides the correct action needed to play the guitar.

Neck Press - gentle heat and pressure used to straighten a neck.

Nut - located at the end of the fingerboard before the headstock, used to provide proper string height and spacing before the strings enter the tuners.

P

P-90 - an early Gibson single coil pickup.

PAF - a sticker on Gibson pickups.

Passive - a guitar that does not use pickups which require power (active pickups).

Peghead - where the tuners are mounted, also called a headstock.

Pickguard - also called a scratchplate, a thin covering screwed or glued to the top of a guitar to protect the guitar from picks and fingernails. Comes in a variety of colors and styles. Often cracked around the screw holes on vintage guitars.

Pot - a Potentiometer mounted to the body of an electric guitar commonly used for control of volume and tone. The tone pot will normally have a CAP soldered in circuit.

Pre-CBS - Fender guitars manufactured before the 1965 takeover of Fender by CBS. Vintage collectors prefer pre-CBS guitars.

Q

Quilted - beautiful undulating patterns found in wood, generally refers to Maple and can also be referred to as "maple quilting" or maple quilted".

R

Relief - upward arching bow in an instrument's neck that allows the strings to move without touching the frets. A bowed or warped neck will have to be heated and pressed to restore the neck to correct relief.

Refin - a refinished guitar. Refinished guitars have a significantly lower value than original guitar with the original surface.

Refret - also called a fret job, refers to re-fretting a guitar.

Rout - a hole or cavity cut into a guitar, often the body of the guitar. Many times a pickup cavity is routed to enable a different pickup to be installed. Routing will diminish the value of a vintage guitar and routing should not be done on a valuable guitar.

Rosette - The decorative strip or inlay work found around the soundhole on an acoustic guitar.

S

Saddle - the part of the bridge where the strings make contact transferring the string vibration to the bridge and body of the guitar.

Scale Length - length of the vibrating string from nut to saddle or twice the distance from the nut to the 12th fret.

Set Neck - a neck that is glued into the body and uses no bolts for attachment.

Single Coil Pickup - an early pickup design with a single coil of wire wrapped around a magnet.

Solid Body - refers to electric guitars with a solid (non-hollow) body.

Sound Hole - hole in the top of the body of a hollow body guitar. May enhance sound of be simply for looks. An F-Hole is a type of sound hole.

Sustain - Length of time a string vibrates

Split Coil - a double coil pickup wound with multiple coils that are smaller than a standard 2 coil pickup where each coil works with a few strings.

Stop Tailpiece - also called a stud tailpiece. Fixed to the top of the guitar and anchors the strings to the top. Holes in the tailpiece allow strings to pass thru the stop tailpiece and over the bridge.

T

T- Frets - the shape of the metal fret. T-Frets are used in most refrets.

Tailpiece - on instruments without bridge pins the strings are commonly anchored to a tailpiece. This normally mounts to the end block and pulls the strings down towards the top after passing across the bridge.

Thinline - hollow body electric guitars, first used with the Gibson Byrdland guitar.

Through Neck - a Thru neck design uses a neck that actually runs right thru the middle of the body.

Trapeze Tailpiece - tailpiece design that has a hinge like mechanism on it and has a shape similar to a swinging trapeze.

Tremolo - another term used for Vibrato or Tremolo Arm

Truss Rod - a rod that runs through the middle of a guitar's neck below the fingerboard. The truss rod helps to stiffen the neck and prevent bowing caused by the tension caused by the strings.

Truss Rod Cover - a decorative cover that covers up the access point for adjusting the truss rod.

Thumbwheel - a small wheel used on adjustable bridges (those usually found on archtop guitars or mandolins) to adjust the bridges height. The top portion of an adjustable bridge rest upon these flat wheels and as they are screwed upward on their post the top portion of the bridge is raised.

Tune-o-matic - this bridge is commonly found on Les Paul style electric guitars. It sits on two thumbwheels and has six saddles which allow individual intonation adjustment for each string.

Tuning Machines - mechanical devices used to increase or decrease string tension.

V

Veneer - thin wood or plastic laminate used in the construction of some guitars.

Vibrato – the bridge and/or tailpiece which can alter the pitch of strings when the vibrato arm is pressed. Also called a whammy bar.

Volute - a piece of wood installed just behind the peghead. It strengthens the neck where the headstock begins.

Index

Index

Index

Above: Blackbird Rider acoustic guitar